Notes From

a

Lesser Reality:

metaphysical essays

KINGSLEY L. DENNIS

BEAUTIFUL TRAITOR BOOKS

Published by Beautiful Traitor Books –

http://www.beautifultraitorbooks.com/

ISBN-13: 978-1-913816-80-3 (paperback)

First published: March 2023

Cover Concept: Kingsley L. Dennis & Ibolya Kapta

Cover & Interior Design: Ibolya Kapta

info@beautifultraitorbooks.com

INTRODUCTION

'We shall no doubt survive the twentieth century; but unless there are great changes, few will survive the twenty-first.'

J.G. Bennett

Such were the prophetic words of the English philosopher and teacher J.G. Bennett spoken over half a century ago. We can no longer afford to turn a blind eye or remain in ignorance about the conditions of the world as they have been for a long time. Especially now when there are agendas in play to not only sustain these conditions but to extend them further contrary to a tide of necessary development. There is a revolution happening in world affairs; yet unfortunately, this revolution is not a renewal but a suppression of those aspects necessary for coherent human evolvement. The shift into an increasing materialism is keeping the human being deeply enveloped in earthly life, severed from aspects of the inner being and the interior gaze. The technological revolution unfolding ever more rapidly across the globe includes the cleverly orchestrated roll-out of a systematic, and institutionalized, procedure of predictive programming, thought-control, and strategies to establish a new consensus reality. Each generation, yet the younger ones especially, are being compelled and persuaded (i.e., recalibrated and processed) into adapting to a mechanized existence. For the lesser few – those with eyes *to see* and ears *to hear* – there is another, alternative pathway to take. It is a pathway of the inner gaze and attention, of stepping through the world without being entangled within the world.

As the opening quote from Bennett states, there was significant concern for humanity's future going into the third millennium. We survived the stormy twentieth century by what seemed like the skin of our teeth. Even at the turn of the new millennium, the future appeared foreboding. Those teachings that were made public during the last century were done so in order to prepare people not only for their current situation but more so for the times to come. And humanity is in those times right now.

As any attentive person can see, humanity is not in its right place. There is still much to be done to heal our polarizations, fragmentations, and splintering. Life within the exterior world of distraction and dissonance keeps us drowsy and in slumber. When slumbering we are also splintered within ourselves. To redress this state of fracture and fragmentation we require awareness, attention, intention, will, and energy. These are the

2

basic necessities for the pathway out of the entrapment of the lesser reality. The essays gathered together in this collection were written for that very purpose. As it is said, real knowledge can only begin where one's own sense of understanding ends.

PART ONE – ESSAYS 2021

'People of Western culture put great value on the level of
a man's knowledge but they do not value the level of a
man's being and are not ashamed of the low level of their
own being. They do not even understand what it means.
And they do not understand that a man's knowledge
depends on the level of his being.'

P.D. Ouspensky, *Fragments of an Unknown Teaching*

BLINDSIDED

*'The real tragedy of our time lies not so much in the
unprecedented external events themselves as in the
unprecedented ethical destitution and spiritual infirmity which
they glaringly reveal.'*

Paul Brunton

Several years ago, I used the same opening quote when I
was writing about what I called a 'metaphysical malaise.'
As I observed the general outer events, I felt it was
evident that they revealed an inner lack. I also added a
second quote from Paul Brunton: 'when political relations
become an elaborate façade for hiding the spiritually
empty rooms behind them, menacing problems are sure
to appear on every side.' Both this quote, and the opening
citation, were published in 1952 and yet they also describe
our current situation today. Another way to state this is to
say that many people have become 'internally numbed'
by what they see occurring in the world, and feel that only
a similar harsh, physical response can be effective. That

is, the inner lack is being compensated for by an extreme swing to external actions and acceptance of authoritarian measures from governing systems. The crisis of our times is that our societies do not consider human purpose and the deeper meaning of human existence. Dark pathways will always emerge and grow in the places where the light is flickering without focus or intent.

The world today is increasingly fragmented. The current global situation is triggering a collapse of the body – individual, social, and psychological. The collective social mind too is in trauma, and the body is showing this illness or dis-ease. Our modern economic-driven societies were already collapsing when the 'bio-agent' came along to accelerate the process. We are now being impacted not only by the forces around the bio-agent but also an info-virus and a psycho-virus. Our social mind and body are collapsing morally and spiritually. We are walking unguided through a new landscape of anxiety. We are being blindsided by what I see as the "bullfighter effect" – this is where the bullfighter keeps the bull blinded and fixated by the cape. The bull twists, turns, and runs, yet always their vision is narrowed onto the cape that is always placed right in front of their nose. Similarly, people live their lives blinded by a cape they never comprehend. We are being cajoled and coerced into chasing the cape, and because of this our vision is narrowed and we are unable to see the bigger picture. People are fighting between themselves for scraps of the cape. Yet we are not seeing those who are the holding the capes – those disguised as the bullfighters. Our societies, our cultures, and our very humanity is being recoded. We are being recoded biologically, socially, and psychologically. The biological and psychological dimension has coalesced to the detriment of our inner life – the life of the spirit.

If this continues, then we shall have allowed ourselves to be drawn into a collective, and individual, state of impotence – physically and psychologically. It is the IMPOTENCE OF WILL. The writer-philosopher Colin Wilson recognized the beginnings of this decades ago: he referred to this predicament as the *insignificance fallacy*. It is now an attitude that is permeating more and more of our modern societies – a general sense of *insignificance*. The insignificance fallacy is promoted by increased materialism and strengthened by strategies of fear that beholden people to seek external security. There is a lack of inner direction as there is simultaneously a rise in 'other-directed' societies. And yet, other-directed societies finally lead to a 'tyranny of the majority.' This can be said to be the actual fate of so-called 'democracies.' The repression against inner-direction (human sovereignty) can unwittingly create societies where a loss of meaning produces a moral and ethical void. And in such a void, society imposes a pressure to become a 'good member of society' and join the consensus – the 'tyranny of the majority.' Even social movements that emerge in such societies (whether ecological or based on social identities) usually show a lack of inner-direction and people unknowingly act more as converts rather than sovereign individuals. Such people tend to often depend on external authority as guidance even when they believe the contrary.

What is required now, I would propose, is a *deepening of internal experience*. The inner-directed person can empty their hands and still hold everything. Inner-direction is not an end purpose but an ongoing means. Inner-direction is not an influence through mass-mindedness, or a blindsided obedience without questioning. Turning inward is the first step toward genuine freedom. It forms a detachment from the distractions of an external reality in order to more clearly perceive the nuances of reality. It is a deepening of subjectivity in order to have more clarity and objectivity.

Humanity is now engaged in a profound moment along its future path. Whether it is recognized or not, we are each living and participating in a reality that exists upon profound metaphysical principles. That's the bottom line. We can choose to participate in this metaphysical reality, consciously and willingly, or be coerced through our lives unbeknown and under influence to external forces that impel us.

"It is slavery or freedom...Without integrity, there's no civilization. So, if you want to be part of something that has integrity, you can't stay [in the old system]. I say it again,

there's no middle of the road...But you have to choose integrity and civilization or choose being a slave of organized crime. You have to make that choice." (Catherine Austin Fitts)

The Sovereign Self

*When you are with your sovereign Self, you can then walk in
the noise again and show people that silence is here too, in your
very own being. When you act forth from your Being – your
Self – you ground the energy within you.
You can be the quiet within the noise.*

Kaleb Seth Perl
Own Your Sovereignty

According to Prof. Mattias Desmet, psychotherapist and
Professor of Clinical Psychology at Ghent University,
mental health in our modern societies has been declining
for decades. This is indicated, he says, by a steady increase
in the number of depression and anxiety issues and the
number of suicides. One of the consequences of this, in
recent years, is the 'enormous growth in absenteeism due
to psychological suffering and burnouts.'[1] This malaise,
we are informed, was growing exponentially even before
the pandemic outbreak of 2020. What this suggests is that
there was already a great deal of trauma being experienced
within people and within many of our human cultures in
the preceding years (as I explored in my book 'Healing the
Wounded Mind' 2019). Prof. Desmet suggests that these
findings indicated that 'society was heading for a tipping

point where a psychological "reorganization" of the social system was imperative.' In other words, we were, broadly speaking, ripe for a tipping into a new direction one way or another. And the direction we were to be 'tipped into' would depend upon the nature of the trigger, how it would be applied, and its related features.

There was already a strong latent apprehension, nervousness and anxiety in many human populations before the 'health crisis' landed upon our shores. The reactions of the political establishments, the media, and related organizations that had a vested interest in steering the situation, aroused further fear and panic amongst the people rather than reassuring them (as would have been their role). When a situation is turned into a crisis, it is then only a small further step to turn a crisis into a trauma. When the trauma is related to an expanded event – such as on a global level – then the very nature of that trauma is no longer an isolated experience but a continual process. Furthermore, a continual traumatic process only needs nudges placed at varying intervals to maintain, and sustain, the traumatic experience. The danger in this is that such an experience can be prolonged almost indefinitely if the nudges continue to be applied. In such psychological states, it becomes very hard for a person to maintain, and act from, their sovereign self for they have become increasingly *externalized* and pulled into (or entangled in) a shared traumatic experience.

Another issue to consider is that of transference of suffering and blame. Prof. Desmet points out, and he is not alone in this, that there already existed in our societies a 'widespread psychological suffering, lack of meaning, and diminished social ties.' When the health crisis got expanded into a structure of biosecurity, many people transferred their existent anxieties and blame onto the dominant health narratives. Fear and discomfort were no longer a result of how modern societies have been structured, along with their attendant political and economic power systems, but rather is now due to a health issue. In this transference of blame, many people naturally wanted to eradicate this source of their suffering and so were ready to point their fingers in the direction where the dominant narratives told them. 'Help us get rid of this health menace' they cried out and fell into line obediently. It pains me to point this out, but such tactics of 'transference of blame' were used to devastating effect by National Socialism in the first half of the twentieth century. And we now know where that led to.[2]

Authoritarian policies applied from the top down appear to bring some form of social solidarity to the situation – yet this is a fallacy. I have referred to this as the *normalization of delusion*.[3] On the contrary, I would state that there is a great deal of 'deliberate fracturing' going on in our societies. Part of this is due to a narrowing of peoples' focus onto a small fragment of the situation at the expense of perceiving the bigger picture (see my previous essay 'Blindsided').[4] This orchestrated narrowing of focus breaks up overall awareness into fractals – into 'reality bubbles.' Since the narrowed focus is directed, by the mainstream media narratives, onto the 'let us get well again' scenario, then people are persuaded into accepting a loss of freedoms and liberty in order to be seemingly granted this. The narrative of 'optimising public health' comes at a cost of increased loss of personal privacy and sovereignty. It is no longer a health issue but rather one of social management. Yet any questioning of this is immediately turned into a questioning of public health. Naturally, any sensible person wishes for public health and well-being, which is why any critical questioning gets censored as a rejection of health that is harder to defend amongst the media-programmed masses. People are turned against one another, and social alliances break down. This, as I have said, is part of a strategy of 'deliberate fracturing.' Prof. Desmet makes a valid point when he states that: 'people cannot be healthy, either physically or mentally, without sufficient freedom, privacy and the right to self-determination.'[5] What this amounts to, says Prof. Desmet, is not a health crisis but a social and cultural crisis. I would add to this that it amounts to a human spiritual crisis too. Taken all together, we are in the midst of a profound turning point for humankind. The core question now is in which direction will humanity take from here on?

What we need, as individuals as well as collectively, is a degree of perception and awareness to *see* and *understand* that relations between things on the surface are not the same as the realities that lie underneath. Surface fragmentations are a construct that have been established to break certain social cohesions. This is because a lack of social cohesion will inevitably strengthen the hand of the authorities. For this reason, great pressure has been applied onto censorship in the media. Solidarity groupings that question the main narratives are either ignored or blatantly censored and suppressed. Gatherings of people who come together in cohesion and shared alliances against the main narratives will not be seen in the mainstream media. Rather, the narrow focus will be maintained upon the narratives of anxiety and division. This is because it is 'these fracturing, surface relations that will draw you out from yourselves, into your programmed-social selves, and away from the underlying cohesions beneath...[6]

The strategy here is to gain power over people by dividing their cohesion and splintering the energies of solidarity and togetherness. As writer Kaleb Seth Perl puts it: '*This is a heist against innate human sovereignty.*' And I would agree with this. Our awareness is being taken away from those things that bring us together and onto those elements that splinter us apart. And this is an affront upon the human sovereign self. Kaleb Seth Perl goes on to say that: 'All kinds of things are being falsely presented to you now to deflect you from the knowledge of the situation. You are now living in the age when human beings must take affairs back into their own hands.'[7] In other words, it is time to *own your sovereignty.*

16

And as an initial step in this process, we can disengage with the distractions, dissonance, and noise and turn the gaze inward to focus on our sovereign Self. We should not allow the mainstream narratives to entangle us in our social personas, naïvely being pulled along by divisive media tales and propaganda. We should take our steps from a place of grounded balance. We need to view the situation – the bigger picture – from a perspective that transcends the controlled narratives.

As the opening quote from Kaleb Seth Perl says, we can be 'the quiet within the noise.' And from this place of centeredness, we can be connected to our own source of energy, wholeness, and resonant balance. It is only from such a place can we then make the right decisions about our life and the future we wish for us and for all.

1   https://dailysceptic.org/interview-with-mattias   desmet-professor-of-clinical-psychology/

2   See Hannah Arendt's The Origins of Totalitarianism

3   See my previous book Hijacking Reality

4   https://kingsleydennis.com/blindsided/

5   https://dailysceptic.org/interview-with-mattias-desmet-professor-of-clinical-psychology/

6   Kaleb Seth Perl, Own Your Sovereignty (New Revolutions Publishing, 2020)

7   Kaleb Seth Perl, Own Your Sovereignty (New Revolutions Publishing, 2020)

The Establishment of Mass Psychology & False Solidarity

It is always necessary to critically question our assumptions and the information that informs our social behaviour. In this essay, I will cast a glance over how current social manifestations have been redefining our social patterns and relations. I will also be examining these patterns from the perspectives of mass psychology, mental intoxication, and a reprogrammed solidarity. According to Prof. Mattias Desmet,[1] the four conditions that allow mass formation – popularly referred to as crowd psychology – to emerge are: a lack of social bonds; people experiencing life as meaningless or senseless; free-floating anxiety; and free-floating frustration and aggression. In recent years, and even going back decades, these conditions have been

• • • • • • • • • • • •

1 Psychotherapist and Professor of Clinical Psychology at Ghent University

building up within our modern societies. As I mentioned in a previous essay,[2] social anxiety and psychological suffering were already growing exponentially even before the pandemic outbreak of 2020. The foundations for establishing a mass psychology were existent in many, if not most, of our industrialized societies and cultures before the traumatic experience of the current pandemic. At such junctures of psychological vulnerability, a shift of attachment – that is, a transference of identification – can be achieved rapidly. What has likely occurred within the past 2 years has been a widescale process of reprogrammed solidarity.

Prof. Mattias Desmet believes the world has experienced a huge, global ritual that has established a new form (a recalibrated form) of social bonding. Desmet also states that this newly arrived mass psychology is a manner of compensation for many years of extreme individualism where people felt they needed to seek out new and different collective bonds of solidarity. This new solidarity frees people from their prior isolationism and atomization. It is a socially programmed and managed method of social re-gathering. And it is being accomplished on a worldwide scale. Also, it is brought into being through a form of ritual. Rituals are not only for religious or sacred circumstances. By definition, a ritual is 'a sequence of activities involving gestures, words, actions,

. . . .

2 https://kingsleydennis.com/the-sovereign-self/

or objects, performed according to a set sequence.'³ That is, they are a range of actions performed according to a prescribed order. And that 'prescribed order' can come through agreement or imposition – or a mixture of both. Participation in rituals also develop a degree of loyalty to the group/grouping through adherence to and the performing of acts that support the main narratives. These acts of obedience (behaviour sets) can be regarded as rituals, similar to how more familiar religious rituals are performed to denote loyalty to a specific religious faith. When social acts are performed through an emotional attachment of ritual, a form of 'hypnotic allegiance' is established that is then extremely hard to break away from. This can then lead to a form of misplaced ethics that can cause people to engage in acts of self-sacrifice in order to uphold what they have been led to believe is their ethical position. People caught up within the mass hypnosis are made to sincerely believe that the mainstream narratives are correct and that they are right to be following and supporting them – even when the evidence points to the contrary. In other words, such people strongly believe in the moral rightness of their position, and this gives them a more powerful sense of solidarity and justification. Similarly, during the Crusades each side felt they were doing 'God's work' by engaging in mass slaughter. What we see here is a condition of misplaced ethics.

People swept up within a mass or crowd

. . . .

3 https://en.wikipedia.org/wiki/Ritual

psychology tend to protect and maintain it whether consciously or unconsciously. This is why they are most likely to reject any contrary information when it is presented to them; or will reject even the chance for such information to be presented. This amounts to a state of mild induced hypnosis which has shifted from an external identification to a self-maintained state. That is, people engage in the process of their own induced hypnosis. This may sound implausible to some people, yet we need to observe the conditions that were present to allow such states of hypnosis. Part reason for this is that many of the people who accepted the slippage into the formation of a mass psychology were already experiencing psychological discontent. This could come from perceiving a lack of life purpose and meaning; a dislike of their jobs; general restlessness and anxiety; and similar issues related with their previous life status. In such cases, the way to break the hypnosis is not by trying to persuade such people to return to their 'old normal' ways, which they were not happy with previously, but by searching out ways to alleviate the source of their psychological discontent. And this suggests a radical transformation in our social and cultural systems and ways of living. Furthermore, it points to a shift away from increasing materialism, automation, and technological dependency into a path that celebrates more the beauty and meaning in being human.

Mass Hypnosis of Solidarity

Persons susceptible to mass psychology are less likely to be responsive or sensitive to rational argument and debate. It is because they did not fall into line with the main narrative through reasoning but rather through a form of 'mental intoxication' that triggered a transference of social bonding to the newly established mass solidarity. Such triggers are generally most effective when they are presented through emotional states – these are often based upon fear; (in)securities; and mortality. When such fear-related triggers are heightened and expanded through widescale media coverage, then most, if not all, alternative narratives are discredited, discarded, and ignored. When within such heightened emotional states, cognitive decisions become overruled by inter-personal circumstances. Importantly, the state-supported narrative (the new consensus) gives people an object to connect their anxiety with. They have a mental representation of what is the cause of their anxiety. Their previous condition of free-floating anxiety has now become anchored, and people feel they are then better able to control their frustrations. To take away their belief in the dominantly imposed narrative would confront the person with their initial unease and psychological discontent. For this reason, it is difficult to break or stop such collective psychological formations once they have been established. Once the psychological patterning and emotional identification has been constructed it is then difficult to deconstruct – a significant collective solidarity has been established that imprints the mass mind.

Another factor that strengthens the mass psychology is that the imposed mainstream narratives appear to speak in one collective voice. They are clearer in what they represent and appear to come from a place of unified agreement (i.e., all state actors and state-affiliated actors are showing public agreement). It is important that there is no public disagreement on the narratives. This sense of external clarity further strengthens the issue as a ritualistic act – a hypnotic formation. The other voices that speak out against the dominant imposed narratives are not regarded or seen as coherent because they speak in many, varied voices. This is usually because they come from many and varied sources that have liberty to say things in different ways. Yet this seeming lack of narrative coherency is weaker at confronting or opposing the hypnotic collective. Those people who remain uncertain and not yet fully decided are then more liable to choose the 'crowd narrative' because the mass storyline falsely appears as more solid. Those people caught within the mass programming believe themselves to be expressing their own opinions when in fact there has been a clever sleight-of-hand in that they have been provided with a set of pre-formed 'opinion bundles' that they can then put forward as their own. Such people are therefore not expressing personal opinions arrived at through individual critical questioning but rather conditioned 'thought bundles' provided through the programming techniques built into the establishment of the psychological collective mass. The mass hypnosis of solidarity comes with a pre-prepared collection of opinion sets for bulk dispersal. However entrenched this situation appears, there is always the possibility for counteracting the collective hypnosis.

Regathering our Unity

It is important that those people who see, perceive, and understand the contradictions and falsity in the mass narratives continue to speak out. Hypnosis can be lessened or weakened through continual exposure to rational information, even when that information opposes the narratives of the mass psychology.

The first step in countering the mass psychosis is to disconnect people's anxiety from the 'object' that people were persuaded to transfer their identification to. This can be understandably difficult when the mainstream media is not at your availability but is working to maintain the hypnotic imprinting of the mass narratives. One way, however, that works to make this disconnect is by presenting a scenario – an 'object threat' – that may be greater than the one used in the original collective imprinting. For example, if people realized that the current 'health crisis' could lead to a condition of totalitarianism, then this realization could be sufficient to awaken people from their hypnosis as they still have the cognitive capacity to grasp that the social condition of totalitarianism is a graver threat than a biological agent with low mortality rate.

The real issues, and the one that creates a fertile ground for inducing a mass psychology in the first place, is the lack of social bonding in our societies and a perceived lack of meaning. This perceived lack of meaning and purpose in everyday life is what produces the feeling of 'free-floating' anxiety. The danger here is that a populace under the sway of mass psychology – mass induced hypnosis – is more likely to support or go along with a totalitarian regime that maintains this mass hypnosis. This was one of the reasons why Germany's National Socialism (the Nazi regime) was so successful in its aims.

The people who were less susceptible to hypnosis of mass psychology tended to be those who disagreed with the ideology behind it or had more experience in using critical analysis of social phenomena, and/or were more aware of the processes of social conditioning and the uses of mainstream propaganda. They were much more capable of spotting from the onset how the narratives of the mass psychology were treating people as mere biological units to be moved around the chess board. The question that now needs to be asked is: how can those people who stand apart from the mass hypnosis be able to unify? Those who can speak out against the mass hypnosis need to connect together. And their advantage is that they are unified through an understanding whilst remaining diverse in their backgrounds, belief structures, identities, etc. Such people can find cohesion in perspectives whilst remaining as diverse and independent individuals. This diversity and individual independence bring greater strength than a collective mass that has been unified through the programming of a false solidarity.

It is important that those people with perceptive cognition recognize that a global ritual has been set into motion that has as its goal the 'retraining' of the populace into welcoming upon them a new civilizational model. The willing compliance to adopt this new model of order, at the local, regional, national and global level, will sever humanity from its own biological and constitutional roots. In order to move forward as human beings, we will likely need to reject certain materialistic futures offered to us. These offers will come with promises of comfort and convenience; yet they will hide an underbelly of human disconnect and the loss of the human spirit. If a deal is made with the devil, then we can be sure that our souls will be collected without delay. And the great truth that gives humanity its strength is that the human soul and spirit can never be taken without our willing compliance. In that, by denying them our willing compliance we strengthen our unity by default. The unity established through conscious awareness is always greater energetically than the perceived unity through unconscious programming. If the fewer are aware, and conscious of what is being attempted by the mass hypnosis, then this shall energetically give us a stronger unity. And the way to break the mass hypnosis is by aligning with a greater truth that shall gradually resynch and recalibrate the energetic vibration of the collective.

The Threshold of Exhaustion: Our Time for Regathering & Recalibration

Decades of expansionist practices and beliefs have brought us to a new threshold. It is not yet the threshold between human and spirit, as some would have preferred, but a threshold of exhaustion.

The modern age of post-industrialization has been feeding an acceleration cycle that is built upon continual expansion and consumption. These expansionist policies are mostly a result of the neo-capitalist thirst for ever increasing profits. And these ever-increasing returns have been predicated upon continuous wars, expanded trading (e.g., globalization), and the ongoing patterns of consumption. Modern world expansion has plundered and exhausted the world's physical resources and has exploited the nervous system of humanity, bringing it to a psycho-fragility and biological burnout. The global brain is entering a state of dementia at the same time it is encountering competition from the automated global brain. This current human, and yet inhumane, thrust have brought the present generations to a threshold of exhaustion. We have saturated our limits of attention and are becoming quickly overwhelmed by the smallest of impacts. The human psyche is becoming over-sensitive to environmental stimuli that is now bombarding us from every media channel we can cram onto our devices. Humanity has forged a new environment for itself within the last century – and especially in the last decades – that pushes us further away from a natural context and towards an artificial, unnatural construct. Many people, or at least those within industrialized cultures, are now perceiving reality from within a bubble of stimulation. An overload of images, sounds, pixels, digitization, and the real-time 'always on' lifestyles that now wrap around us have created an unprecedented level of electromagnetic smog. We have slipped into an electronic ecosystem without being consciously aware of what was happening until we were already embedded deeply within it. This new electrocuted environment shifts humans from a state of self-perception into a mode of info-stimulation. Our minds and bodies are being re-tuned and recalibrated to exist within a state of permanent excitement.

Human life is now for many people an experience of hyper-expression. The human inner life is being pulled out of us and sprawled upon the external chaotic mediascape. No wonder we are witnessing so many cases of nervous system exhaustion. Our nervous systems are being exploited until the point of near explosion. The sad part here is that a medical industry has been established to cater to this by profit-centred chemicalization of our bodies and minds. It is no longer the jagged pill we should be cautious of but the plethora of smooth pills we are constantly offered that many people are only too willing to pop. The human nervous system (the body-mind) has reached a point of saturation: too much noise, too many nervous stimulations, too much vibrational dissonance: people are quite literally cracking up. There is a subtle state of traumatization that has entered as a low-level hum within our global vibration. Many people have become entrained into this hum. It is creating an underlying sense of anxiety, unease, uncertainty, and restless nervousness. Something is afoot. Many of us feel this, and yet cannot quite place it. There is a presence in the room – yet it is out of visible sight. A moment of regathering is now required.

A moment of regathering is necessary as individually and collectively we are becoming out-of-synch with our vibrational alignment. Technology has created some of this dissonance, although not all. Over the years, humanity has been given nudges to assist its re-alignment. But now, something stronger is required: 'you have not been inclined to feel that nudge. Now, it has to be more so of a blow rather than a nudge.'[4] As a species we are not yet sufficiently unified, or connected, to be making

. . . .

4 (S.5.Q11)

the best use from technology. We can see this clearly from the behaviour we witness online and in social media. We are still too splintered for our technologies to be of most use to us. If we are not aligned, then there is the danger that any technologies we develop will create further dissonance and dysfunction. Humanity needs to respond to this situation, but by awareness and vibrational re-alignment, and not by taking itself further away from life: 'it is never about ridding life of yourselves: sitting upon a hilltop void of self, void of world, no.'[5] What we need is to strip it all away – to strip back our socially constructed lives into a way of living that is closer to the essential. We need to allow the expansive vibrational essence to flow through us: 'allow this vibrational essence to flow through your being, birthing a new vibrational signature - a non-splintered one, a unified one.'[6] Humanity needs to take off its bandages and to allow its wounds to heal. It is time to shift into a more harmonized species vibration; this is crucial now. A more aligned and vibrationally resonant humanity can emerge from this – 'one consciousness at a time, one vibrational alignment at a time.' And this is where human beings can be of purpose, both physically in their everyday lives and in alignment with the resonance of pure consciousness.

Human life is also about the expanding of our field of consciousness; to allow pure consciousness to manifest

. . . .

5 (S.5.Q11)

6 (S.5.Q11)

through the physical human being. The physical being is biologically encased, yet this does not mean that we should be encased in our limitations of consciousness. Humanity has already explored far and wide. We have gone deep into the oceans, far across the Earth, and high up into the atmosphere and into orbit. Yet if we don't explore and reach ourselves first, then we shall have found nothing: 'You can only ever but find yourselves. But if so coming from a splintered mind, you are finding everything else but yourselves.'[7] It is time to unclose the closed; to reveal the unrevealed. How can we be going towards the "post-human" if we have not yet arrived at the *fully human*? By coming back to our essential selves, new pathways shall open up for us – a new resonance shall be gained. A new sight shall be revealed: 'they will be new to the eyes that have not yet been open but old news to those that have been awake.'[8] The human is both within *being* and *becoming* – between stillness and movement. This is the flow of evolution and has always been so. Consciousness has always been in flow through humanity, yet it manifests in relation to the pathways that have been created. It is now time for new pathways to be established, so that pure consciousness can flow more abundantly. It is time now for a genuine human recalibration into a consciousness vibration – not into an artificial electro-smog vibration.

. . . .

7 (S.5.Q14)

8 (S.5.Q15)

By recalibrating and re-wiring, then we are also dropping old patterns (patterning) and habits. As connections and patterns are internally shifted, so too will this affect our outer lives. To shift the outer, we must first shift the inner: 'opening up for new pathways to be formed which are more of resonation to your being and to that of which is trying to manifest in form.'[9] This is our moment for regathering and recalibration. It is the time for a readjustment and return to humanity's home resonance. It is time for all of us to find *The Way Back Home*. We have been taught to be in a constant struggle of extremes; to be thrust between spurts of action and sudden, constant rest. In this way, we are actually flat-lining life: 'You are straightening it out, and also it goes for the other end of constant rest. It has to be of resonance - of movement, of rest, of breath.'[10] The energy is always there, available for us, only that it needs to be in resonance to the 'mechanism or organism that is receiving such vibrations.' And right now, the human organism requires some recalibration so that more expanded energy, consciousness, and awareness, can come forth through us. If a person is in dissonance, out of balance with themselves, rather than align with the energies of expanded consciousness they will more likely be sucked into the ecosystem of electro-energies. These energies are sub-nature. They are part of living existence, yet they are a lower form of life vibration. Electricity, said Rudolf Steiner, is light in a *sub-material* state. That is, it is

. . . .

9 (S.5.Q19)

10 (S.5.Q23)

a form of light that has fallen below the level of nature and has become what he termed 'sub-nature.' It is because of this that Steiner warned humankind to be cautious not to build cultures dependent or based on electricity. An electro-ecosystem will only serve to draw us away from our natural eco-system and into a lower vibrational state of sub-nature.

Modern living, as we can bear witness to, has desensitized many of us to natural energies of Nature. And the shift into increased digitization has only emphasized this. To attune ourselves to natural, vital life-forces we need to become closer to our natural environments. We need to spend more time outside, being in touch with the soil – to let our hands and feet be grounded by earthly energies. We shouldn't be afraid of earthly dirt or the bacteria in the soil; not to be squeamish at the stains of bugs. What we need is an openness to a state of receptivity and rebalance. We have to make time for *allowance* – to allow ourselves to Be, to be present, and to be receptive to life's vital forces. In this way, we can begin to overcome our collective desensitization and to allow the finer vibrational energies of the vital life-forces to flow through us into this beautiful world we have the privilege of experiencing.

By reaching the threshold of exhaustion, we can now take this opportunity to cross over into a different threshold – a threshold into a new phase where the human being merges with the vital life-forces of pure consciousness. A new phase is incoming. We only have to be balanced, stable, and in-synch for this new allowance.

Endnotes

All citations (listed below) were taken from the ABE communications as published in my previous book *UNIFIED: Cosmos, Life, Purpose – Communicating with the Unified Source Field & How This Can Guide Our Lives* and *The Way Back Home: The ABE Conversations* (Vol.1). The reference notes refer to Section 5 and the Question number.

Leaving an Obsolete System Behind

There is no doubt that humanity has entered a new phase along its developmental journey. We are now observing a grand restructuring of human society and its many systems: financial, technological, political, cultural, and more. I have already spoken about how this is creating great discomfort and dissonance for many people. This is inevitable, for great upheavals are rarely smooth or without disturbances and ripples. A new phase is emerging as the current phase is fragmenting; and like two stones thrown into a pond, they each create interference waves that clash. The important point here is *where a person chooses to position themselves*. A new way of life can be brought into being, yet it must be birthed from within the current one as it breaks up. For a time, both worlds will co-exist in the same physical space although <u>they shall</u>

occupy a different energetic space. Where a person can position themselves is to be **in the world** that is emerging yet not **of the world** that is on the way out. Although one phase has ended, there are those groups/agencies who have vested interests in maintaining this world, and they are desperately attempting to re-model it with a new facelift – as a technocracy. There will be a stealthy attempt at a makeover, to present the 'new future' in terms of an artificial, synthetic future. Yet this is not an evolutionary future for humanity. The new emerging world will remain organic, natural, and in biological balance. This is the model that shall come forth – not a false future in shiny metal. We should take heed from the wise words of Buckminster Fuller: "You never change things by fighting the existing reality. To change something, build a new model that makes the existing model obsolete."

We are here now to build a new model whilst existing within the current one that is fast becoming obsolete. The power that the obsolete system, and its rulers, have over us depends upon our state of being (level of frequency) – that is, others can only 'lord it' over us if we are existing energetically (aka, vibrating) at their level. The obsolete system wants for everyone to operate (energetic state) at its lower-level vibratory state. We simply do not go there. We have to secure and protect the most valuable thing to us – our consciousness. In being better prepared for engaging with the changing world I suggest the following five aspects: i) Conscious awareness; ii) Connection; iii) Communication; iv) Creation; v) Comprehension.

i) Conscious Awareness: to be aware of what is happening in the world, including the distasteful aspects, but not to get dragged into or entangled with these events. Awareness is necessary, but only as a tool for self-knowledge – not to acquire more baggage from the world.

ii) Connection: to find and discover other people who are on the 'same wavelength' and who think and perceive like you. Reach out, connect with others, even if you have never previously met. Send them a message online. Share your thoughts – strengthen one another's energy states. Never feel you are alone. There are **always** other people out there who think and feel the same as you do. Older social alliances will be breaking down. Old or existing friendships and bonds will be dissolving. That's okay – find new ones. Re-align your social alliances according to your new state of perception.

iii) Communication: Share your thoughts and ideas with others. State your truths. Let others know what position you have taken. Do not be cowered into silence or anonymity. Allow others to also find you by letting them know your position and feelings. Do not be loud or go around shouting your views; or, worse still, trying to persuade others to take your position. Just be confident to state your ideas when asked and to represent and communicate your own truths when necessary. By communicating your position with the world outside of you, you shall also be strengthening the trust in yourself.

iv) Creation: be creative! Do not allow the events of the world to pacify or nullify you. Do not be impotent to your own potentials just because of external uncertainties. It is precisely at such times of dissolution and renewal that creativity is most needed. Being creative does not only imply from an artistic point of view. Not everyone can be a painter or musician, etc. But genuine creativity is about being resilient and finding new ways to do things. New patterns of lifestyles; different hobbies; learning new skills; preparing yourself physically, mentally, and emotionally. Being creative means being adaptive during moments of change.

v) Comprehension: be understanding of this change and how it is affecting others. Recognize that there will be many conflicting points of view and opinions. Acknowledge that many people will not only choose not to agree with you but that they may even attack your views. Do not let this sway you from your own understanding and your faith and trust in yourself. Understand the full scope of the wider implications and allow others to have their own views so long as this does not impinge or trespass on yours. And if, later on, some people wish to come over to your way of understanding, be gracious to them and not judgmental. We are all learning at our own pace.

Perhaps these five 'C-Ways' will assist as we each move ahead into the paths we have chosen at this time. It is not necessary to have a full picture or to know exactly how the next years will be. For now, it is enough to visualize that you are already in the world you wish to be, only that it hasn't been built yet. You are there, energetically – later will come the physical structures. Imagine there are two boats upon the water, an old sinking one and a new one. Place yourselves on the new one and know that you are there already, even though it looks empty and without a full crew. For if you believe yourself to be remaining on the old, sinking boat you will spend too much of your energies worrying about how it is sinking and running around, desperately seeking for some unknown solutions. Yet knowing that you are already upon the new boat – the new Ark – you will feel more balanced and energized, ready for sailing when the waters become clearer. You are already where you wish yourself to be – it's just that the new structures haven't yet materialized. But energetically – vibrationally – you are already aligned with the new phase of the human path you have chosen.

As Buckminster Fuller also said: "We are called to be architects of the future, not its victims." The new boat has no room for victims, yet plenty of space for those with a new vision for the future.

Phase Change: Moving into a New Space of Existence

'The Abyss has been looking into us for long enough. It is time for us, after becoming as spiritually grounded and metaphysically well-informed as possible, to begin looking back into it, and so come to a deeper understanding of exactly what is being done to us – and maybe even who is doing it.'

Charles Upton

I recently spoke about leaving an obsolete system behind and moving into the energetic space where a new system can emerge. Grand systemic shifts occur as one cycle draws to a close, allowing for a new phase to come into existence. As this happens, the older environment (reality structure) stagnates – the result, in this case, is a deeper fall into materialism, which if continues, eventually comes to a point of fracture. A deepening material reality appears to create a cut off from subtler planes of being and connection. Yet no matter how this feels, it is metaphysically impossible. It is a time, however, for people to become as 'spiritually grounded and metaphysically well-informed as possible,' as stated by Charles Upton. Why? Because the illusion of ordinary life is fast breaking down.

In these times when there is a 'phase change' – from one phase to another – there is greater vulnerability for fragmentation to appear in the dominant reality structure. Some traditions have referred to these as 'cracks in the veil.' I have used the term *consensus reality meltdown*.[11] It appears that at this juncture in our civilizational path, there is a deliberate attempt to diminish our sense of reality – to make people more suggestible and open for programming. Also, to create a psychic numbness and fear. I sense that there is a parallel 'reality system' being put into place that presents a false 'solidification of the world' through a deliberate push for greater materialistic beliefs and faith in technological solutions. Again, this 'solidification' is a façade that hides the 'fissures' that are opening up in our societies and through which psychic forces are pushing their way through. It is critical now that we each maintain a mental balance as we move forward. Also, it is important in these times that we neither stagnate nor fall too much into the uncertainties of chaos: it is now the fine line we seek between these extremes of solidification and stagnation, and chaos and fear. As always, we are called upon to find the straight path between the maelstrom of distraction and dissonance.

• • • • • • • • • • • •

11 See my book Hijacking Reality: The Reprogramming & Reorganization of Human Life

The Mother (the spiritual companion of the Indian sage Sri Aurobindo) once drew an image for a student who asked her to describe the best path to take in their developmental work. The Mother drew a squiggle, and then a straight line through it. We should aim to be on the straight path, she replied. This is a photo of her image:

(Photo taken at Auroville, India, by the author)

The power that others have over us depends on how far we stray from our own inner dependency – our own 'straight path' that lies within. This is the path of our frequency – is it a squiggle or a straight line? We must answer for ourselves.

We are each more than we have been conditioned to think and believe. It is true that we have been held back by our own imposed limitations. Those limitations were part of a previous time. We are in the midst of a new historical moment (and I don't wish to sound dramatic!)

The human transformation, including our social and cultural systems, will only come about from having a realization of the situation we are in. And this includes a realization and perception of ourselves. If we continue to act and behave from the same patterns, then how can we expect to break this continual chain of conditioned limitations? This is how the status quo maintains itself, from perpetuating the same patterns that keep it in place. Any awakening to the perceptual programming we have been under will activate the 'guardians of falsehood' – or, rather, the modern-hooded *Inquisition against Truth*. This modern Inquisition – similar to the religious Inquisition of the Middle Ages – will seek out to suppress any voices of contention against the dominant narrative. Yet, I suggest, we must now have faith in ourselves to speak our own truths. And speaking one's truth usually fuels our own transformation. Upon this shifting ground, change (one way or another) is inevitable.

Change may be uncomfortable at first. This is the energy felt when old patterns are broken in order to be replaced by the new. There are always those people who prefer to deny these changes, and there is great shame in this:

it is much easier to sit back down and numb-out again because people are so afraid to feel, to love, and to live. What a shame! If only they knew that – wow – this is what I can do. I feel hurt but in this I am alive, I am here, I am participating. Such beauty in this realization.[12]

There is much to be said about this form of participation in life – participation in the changes. Genuine human community is wishing for us to form new connections and to come together through this. This is what the social body is for: it is a body that needs for its limbs to work together, harmoniously, and in unity. The human being is a vibrational part of this communication flow: 'the heart is the connector vibrationally and the head is the receiver - just like a phone line. If these are both open to receive then it will be that way.'[13]

The energy of unity amongst us is powerful; so powerful that it could successfully energize a new form of human civilization to emerge. First, however, change *is* coming. People are already feeling the discomfort of this. And for many people, this 'change' is bringing great challenges and forcing them to make life-changing decisions. In whatever way, something huge is coming that will compel people to make their choices – and

• • • • • • • • • • • •

12 UNIFIED: Cosmos, Life, Purpose – S.3.Q27
13 UNIFIED: Cosmos, Life, Purpose – S.3.Q28

to stand by those choices. For my part, I would want nothing more than to be on the right and noble side of human history. Let each person make their decisions with conscious awareness, comprehension, and perceptual understanding. Let us go forth and make 2022 a year for humanity.

The Power of Discernment

At our general level of awareness there is often no perceptible or discernible pattern to the flow of events. Partly this stems from having been conditioned into perceiving a particular dominant reality program. We do not have access to objective reality, although there can be moments and instances when glimpses occur. The phenomenon of miracles is an example of this, when the laws of a reality outside of our own intervene/operate within our subjective reality. Likewise, many ancient tales, fables, allegories, etc, are representations of what we refer to as a 'higher dimension' operating within our own. Such impulses help us, whether we are conscious of it or not, to re-orientate our perception against the indoctrinated programming. What we often take to be reality is in fact only a very thin slice of a much 'bigger picture.'

The act of discernment is an inward one; as such, it requires a disciplined focus. Yet as we have seen, modern societies not only do they not cater to such practices, but they also actively dissuade us from approaching them. The result of this is that people in general do not see – or *feel* – a need for such a discernment. Modern life keeps us occupied and diverted by other pursuits. Unfortunately, it is often the case that 'shock impacts' are required in order for us to shift our attention away from the 'straight path' of normalized living. And we've been living with such a 'shock event' for almost two years now since the outbreak of the pandemic. We could see our current predicament from this perspective: that modern life was in need of a 'crisis point' within its old patterns for there to arise within people the need for *something else*. It is in such moments of deep reflection that an inner realization may occur: the recognition that common (i.e., consensus) culture does not provide sufficient meaning for our lives. That is, there is the lack of any transcendental, metaphysical impulse. An awareness of such lack often occurs in times when there is a noticeable deterioration in social and cultural systems. Such recognition – or *re-cognition* - is not yet dominant among the majority of our modern so-called 'civilized' nations. Yet we are soon reaching that tipping point.

For too long we have been absent from the vale of 'soul-making,' to quote the poet John Keats. And yet the signs have always been there to guide the way. When our early cave-dwelling ancestors first made their handprints upon the walls of their caves they were signalling to the external world: 'I am here – I exist.' The inner spark of the human being was attempting to be heard – to be imprinted onto the outer life. It was an early stage in the expression of an interiorized human consciousness. In each epoch our consciousness perceives and interprets reality in a particular way. How we experience the reality around us influences our perception of it, and vice-versa. This is why our perceptions have always been a target for direct manipulation – it is our reality-sensing software.

As part of our steps toward discernment we can begin by a recognition of the following factors: i) acknowledgement of one's situation and the need for self-development and/or life adjustment; and ii) the need for partial detachment from one's social and cultural conditioning and external influences. By recognizing these two factors a person can make the first step to self-aware discernment. A gradual de-conditioning of the social personality (the *persona*) helps to develop a detached perspective and to see external impacts for what they are. In order to see and think clearly, we need to methodically de-clutter our social personality. Then, and only then, can a conscious step be taken toward inner freedom and genuine liberty. That is, the old patterns must become less determined, dogmatic, and fixed. Then through this space, where old belief patterns have left their moorings, can new perceptions emerge. As this process gradually unfolds it is important that each person stays grounded in the world – in their everyday lives – and not to entertain themselves with amusing fantasies or unwarranted intoxications. Furthermore, it is important to remember that in all we do we should be in harmony and balance, and not in conflict with our everyday life. Our dignity and decency is not in what it has achieved, nor what it is, but in what it can become. And this is a choice each person can make.

Our Choice

As in everything in our lives, we make a choice. When it comes down to basics - which it inevitably must do - then we find that we have a fundamental choice between living a life in Love or in Fear. In other words, if we choose Love then we side with compassion, empathy, creativity, connection, support, sharing, and resilience. And if we choose to align with the Fear then we give ourselves over to control, manipulation, anxiety, and vulnerability – all the expressions of a culture of oppression.

If we ascribe to a life lived as islands of separation, then inevitably we learn (or are conditioned) to place our trust externally upon a range of institutions; these may range from religious, work/career, social, educational, political, etc. And if these institutions fail us then we naturally feel vulnerability, or even betrayed. And yet the truth of the matter is that we betrayed ourselves in the first place by outsourcing our trust. If we live a life relying upon external systems, then we must be prepared to feel distraught should those external systems breakdown. In such times of great transition, such as now, these social institutions are themselves very fragile. Further, many of these systems are now revealing themselves to be corrupt – or being utilized by corrupt human agents. Right now, I would say that we are witnessing the 'great unravelling' of many of our once trusted systems. We are seeing head-on the undoing of many dishonest, unethical, and toxic structures that inevitably can no longer serve our interests. This unravelling is revealing that our sense of vulnerability is partly the dismantling of our false assumptions. And further, that our sense of vulnerability is the fear of letting go. It is important to be open to receiving information, even if it is of the disagreeable kind. Yet in being open to such information does not mean we should adopt a position of fear. We have to make a choice of not accepting, or adopting, these external aspects of fear and toxicity. They do not 'belong' to us.

In knowing this, we are compelled to seek out those experiences that feel real to us, and which can assist us in developing as human beings. If there is a 'truth' to be discerned, then it must surely come not through artificial constructs but through our everyday personal experiences. To understand that which we call the 'self' is only a construct until we can experience it through the revelation brought about by others. Alone, we are unable to 'see' the self – no more than we can see our own faces. And just as we need a mirror in order to view our face, so too do we need other people and experiences in life to be as mirrors to reveal the workings of the inner Self. In the end, it is our participation in life that shall teach us the discernment we need to tell truth from falsehood. No online course or TV program can teach us this. Let us not back away from ourselves – let us invite us closer in.

Revelation or Fear: The Two Scenarios of a Split-Reality

An experience and/or sensation that people are having in greater frequency recently is that of being in a 'different reality' from other people. I have heard it spoken that someone can be standing right next to another person and yet it feels like both are living in a completely different reality. Is this a new human condition – the 'split-reality syndrome'? And if so, what are the principal aspects of these different realities?

On the one hand, there is little doubt that humanity – yes, that means human life upon this planet – is experiencing monumental shifts and disturbances that include such aspects as: earth changes/disruptions, non-linear climatic variations, economic vulnerabilities and fluctuations, national political system failures, geopolitical fractures, infrastructure breakdowns, global power grabs, mind programming, technocratic control systems, and much more. And on the other hand, we are witnessing an immense shift in peoples' awareness, understanding, and perceptual clarity. So, since we are in the domain of discussing 'big shifts' – and this *is* a time for experiencing large themes – let me bring forward two 'big words' to frame this: *Apocalypse & Armageddon.*

These two words have, in recent times, been coming up repeatedly in spoken and written narratives and conversations. And often, they have been used interchangeably. And the reason for this is that on a very general level, both terms are used to refer to an 'end times' destructive event. Both terms, in this broad context, describe an end time, or end of the world, scenario. And with the current state of the world as it today, and its potential future trajectory, it is understandable that people are using these terms in conversation. Yet, for me, they each represent a different aspect of this 'split-reality.' So, I am going to lay out what, for me, these terms represent and how they play into a different reality scenario for each.

The term *apocalypse* comes from ancient Greek (ἀποκάλυψις – apokálypsis) which literally means 'from cover;' that is, a disclosure or revelation of great knowledge. In religious terminology it has been used to denote a disclosure of something very important that was hidden. This may refer to some 'heavenly secrets,' or similar divine disclosures that may bring understanding onto earthly life. Here then, we have a term representing a 'revelation of the veiled.' In such an instance of an apocalypse, we have a moment of individual and/or collective revelation of some hidden or veiled knowledge. Does this match with the term 'Armageddon'?

Armageddon, in ancient Greek is Ἀρμαγεδών, Harmagedon (and in Hebrew is Har Məgīddō) which is the prophesied location of a battle during the 'end times.' Again, the term *Armageddon* is used in a general sense to refer to any 'end of the world' scenario. Yet it has no revelatory significance or suggests any epiphany. It refers to a physical battle, a time of great end times war – the 'war to end all wars.' As we can see, these two terms represent two distinct moments: one is an instance of revelation (apocalypse), and the other is a specific physical 'war to end all wars' (Armageddon). For me, how people use these terms (if they do at all), and also the presence of these terms in the same narrative, signifies this 'split-reality' positioning. In other words, a person can position themselves within a reality of revelation, a time when hitherto hidden knowledge and understandings are revealed to them – a perceptual awakening. Or, a person can perceive themselves to be caught up with a time of physical warfare, disruption, and destruction. For me, one of these realities allows for a refinement of self-awareness, cognition, and comprehension; the other, a densification, entanglement, and potential disturbance of one's cognition and energy state.

Furthermore, the *apocalypse* mode (to call it that) represents, to my understanding, a movement towards something. A person, through revelation, is transitioning toward a perceptual awareness, or space of knowing. And the *Armageddon* mode is more likely to suggest a running away from something – running away from the destruction and devastation of war. Here, these positionings can also be applied to how people are reacting to one or other of possible future 'reality states.' In these days we are being told to 'prepare for what is coming.' Yet what is coming? How can we really know what is going to come – World War 3 or Evacuation Plan Planet Earth by Pleiadeans? It is most likely that we shall meet exactly what we are preparing for. In my short life experience, I have found that we tend to meet reality halfway (most of the time!). So, in this scenario, if we are stockpiling food, digging our bunkers, and fearing for the worst – what I have called the 'Armageddon-pathogen-virus-zombie-endgame' meme[14] – then we're more likely to run into one of those demonic zombies, or an experience affiliated with this energy. A person is more likely to experience fear, confusion, anxiety, uncertainty, etc, if this is what they are preparing against. Because this structure has become their reality set. Reality has a funny way of responding to what's in our heads – yet most often in a way that we were not expecting.[15]

• • • • • • • • • • • •

14 See my book *Hijacking Reality*

15 If you want a depiction of this, find and watch the film Solaris by Andrei Tarkovsky (1972) – or read the original book by Stanislaw Lem (1961).

What we are running away from usually meets us head on, at some point. Just like in our abstract dreams: we are running away from some fear but going nowhere.

The apocalypse-revelation mode, on the other hand, suggests a position of receptibility and openness to unknown potentials, without fear or apprehension, yet with an inner sense of trust. For you see, we cannot run away from ourselves no matter how fast or how hard we try. We can take ourselves to an underground bunker, or to some isolated island – yet we *take ourselves* with us. And 'how' we are is what determines how we experience what is to be and what is to come.

To return to what was said in the opening sentence, we can be standing right next to another person and yet each person is experiencing and living in a different reality – and responding to this accordingly. We can be physically next to them, but we are certainly not *with* them.

Whether we have recognized it, and acknowledged it, or not – reality has split. And it is time to choose our positions. How we take ourselves forward from this moment on will determine what form and arrangement of life, as well as energetic and emotional states, we are going to experience. Not everyone will be a part of our reality – yet many will. We cannot include all people in our reality, for this will be an individual choice to make, just as you will, or have already, made yours. Reality is about alignment. Our experiences have a way of meeting us halfway, or someway, in alignment with our state of being. It might not all be rosy. Discomfort is also a hereditary aspect of change and transition. In whichever way the future unfolds, and no one can say for sure on this, it will be a question of *how* you choose to meet it. And that will depend upon which reality you have stepped into. Is your future going to be a revelation of hidden truths leading to new understandings and life patterns; or are you battle-ready for the war to end all wars? If you're not yet sure, then take a little time to think about it. But not too much time; but do think long and hard. It's going to be a critical choice.

PART TWO – ESSAYS 2022

'At present mankind is undergoing an evolutionary crisis in which is concealed a choice of its destiny.'

Sri Aurobindo

Levels of Perspective:
the discernment of various scales of perception

'The greatest barrier to consciousness is the belief that one is already conscious.'

P.D. Ouspensky

In the light of current events, I was reflecting that it may help to bring some clarity if we can make distinctions between the various scales of perspective. As I had spoken about previously,[16] different individuals can be physically close to one another yet be experiencing a staggeringly different view of reality. Rather than feel antagonism in this, we need to understand that there are levels, scales, of perspective in operation. For the sake of brevity (and clarity), I shall refer to these as the 2D, 3D, and the 4D perspectives.

The 2D perspective is the one that is shared by most people as it forms the main narrative and is the collective consensus reality. This 'reality' is formed by

· · · · · · · · · · · ·

16 See my 'Split-Reality' essay: https://kingsleydennis.com/revelation-or-fear-the-two-scenarios-of-a-split-reality/

early socio-cultural conditioning that is implemented through early family peer structures, kindergarten schooling onwards (and general educational systems), political structures, media programming, law, and all other institutions that also serve to create a national identity. These days, this conditioning is further sustained through globalist programming as in international media and entertainment. It is the dominant narrative propaganda that is propagated through state television and mainstream media (as well as all so-called 'influencers' that are products of the same programming). It is also pushed as the 'polarity program' – the us vs. them; good vs. bad; right vs. wrong; hero vs. villain – that is particularly dominant at this current time. At this level, people see a highly orchestrated and managed singular side story. From this, they are targeted with emotional material (information, images, etc.) to elicit base responses around survival, security, and well-being. The usual range of programming aims to foster fear and dependency, as well as allegiance and national and/or targeted identities. For the people locked into the 2D perspective, it is almost impossible to release them from this by civil engagement and discussion. They have had their opinions 'locked in' and then repeatedly validated, reenforced, and sustained by waves of continual external programming. In other words, they see and think what they have been programmed to see and think. This, unfortunately, has been the basic perceptive level for the majority of people for a very long time. This state of perceptive existence has allowed groupings, nations, and civilizations to rise and fall amidst ever increasing complexification of social management.

The 3D perspective is where a social awakening has occurred. When this happens, people have managed to break away from the programmed consensus reality construct by being exposed to a wider range of information and stimuli, which also strengthens the intuition. This is often accompanied by an inner nudge that something 'is not quite right' with the main narratives. This perspective comes with a critical questioning of events and the drive to see 'behind the curtain.' That is, people have realized there are other identities pulling the puppet strings of the world stage (just as there was an old man behind the curtain pulling the levers of the Wizard of Oz). The 3D perspective often includes a degree of individual research and investigation in the bid to gain an over-arching perspective of the 'bigger picture.' Whilst this perspective is a step back from the myopic programming construct of 2D, it still remains within the reality construct of the physical life experience. The 3D perspective is often accused of being the realm of 'conspiracy theory,' the lunatic fringe, dissidents, mavericks, etc. (what I have previously referred to as 'heretical consciousness').[17] In this view, people are aware that the world is not run the way that it is said to be (i.e., by elected governments). In

• • • • • • • • • • • •

17 Chapter 15 in *Hijacking Reality: The Reprogramming & Reorganization of Human Life*

the 3D perspective, people know about the history and involvement of secret societies, elite groups, trans-national organizations (financial and otherwise), non-accountable control systems, invisible structures of tyranny, the global 'Great Game' chessboard, deep-state structures, parallel governments, black budgets/black projects, global digital surveillance, full spectrum dominance, trauma-based programming, and much more. The 3D perspective understands that there are elite groups vying for global control that are above and beyond national identities and allegiances, and that exterior events in opposition are often working together. It is no longer about Us vs. Them on a flat horizontal plane but rather the Few vs. The Rest from a top-down vertical pyramidal structure of power. Many more people are awakening now to the 3D perspective and realizing that the reprogramming and reorganization of human life upon this planet is fast becoming a reality. Furthermore, that there is a push for a global technocracy that aims to deconstruct the very concept of the human being. For those people with a sense of the 'bigger picture,' the Great Reset Phase 2 has just been put into operation[18]

Now we come to the 4D perspective, which is less easy to clarify through words. The previous perspectives – 2D & 3D – are both products of the physical reality construct. Yet there is another state of perception that traditionally

• • • • • • • • • • • • •

18 See https://winteroak.org.uk/2022/03/09/the-great-reset-phase-2-war/

has belonged to sages, mystics, initiatory wisdom schools, seers, and the like. This is a degree of perception that takes the human senses beyond the reality construct and into states of awareness not currently recognized or acknowledged within a physical life. For the sake of brevity, it can be referred to as a transcendent perspective. This is a level of perspective that recognizes order on a cosmic scale; and how when the 'cosmic wind blows' (so to speak) there are particular eruptions/events that occur upon the planet. In other words, the 4D perspective comprehends the forces that act beyond the physical and planetary realm, and which have been responsible for the lifespan of grand civilizations, evolutionary mutational jumps, geo-physical alterations, electromagnetic/ energetic shifts, patterns in consciousness fields, and more. There is an order to how patterns of existence operate and function. There is an interrelated field of communication that exists, and to which access is possible for all sentient life forms. There is knowledge available that lies beyond the normal ken of understanding. And this is the 'bigger, bigger picture' that views planetary life even beyond that of the elite globalists! Needless to say, the people that have the 4D perspective are very few and far between. What I'm attempting to state here is that we have to realize that we don't know what we don't know. Furthermore, that there is a lot of activity going on upon realms we are not currently aware of. Wildcards are always possible. Just as in the concept of the Matryoshka nesting Russian dolls, there are layers within layers within layers. At the smallest level, understanding is asleep, dormant – the individual is the automaton. At another layer, people have the ability to act with purpose and intention and to change ground level circumstances and events. At another layer still, there is the possibility for intervention at a level unrecognized by most. Still, this should not stop those people with insight and partial understanding from participating in the flows of history.

Let me be clear, this is not a 'solutions' essay. It was my intention to share some thoughts and reflections, albeit brief, upon the discernment of various scales of perception. By having awareness of our range and scope of perspective, as well as our limitations, we may be better positioned to consider the situation and of changing circumstances. As the thinker Paul Brunton said:

> The sturdy struggle of reason against passion, intuition against suggestion, truth against self-interest, individuality against the mass and contemplation against convention is an unending one. But it is also an honourable one...It is both a blunder and a sin to take the easier path.[19]

• • • • • • • • • • • •

19 Brunton, Paul. 1974 (1952). *The Spiritual Crisis of Man*. London: Rider & Company, p42

The Eleventh Hour

In the Age of Materialism, it is said that people have their orientation outwards and towards the boundary that separates humanity from the lower orders – the animals and plants – rather than the inner orientation towards Source. And it is within the great depth of materialism that represents the final stage of a grand cycle where the world reaches its 'extremity of separation' in a period of remoteness from the sacred impulse. Unknowing and blind to this, the materialist believes they experience no loss because progress has given humanity much more than it ever had, and that material progress shall be their salvation. At such a time, it symbolizes that humankind has reached a limit of distance (an extremity) from its essential nature – from its centre – and thus from its sacred home. And the modern person – especially the product of westernized modernism – has gone so far from their essential nature that they have ceased to think of it or question its existence, and even fabricate and invent a pseudo-truth for its material reality. Many now see these times of deep materialism as representing the 'eleventh hour' for humanity; as a decisive moment before a dramatic turn of events in its trajectory. Others, like myself, have referred to these times as representing humanity's 'dark night of the soul.' I wrote the following passage over a decade ago:

We have now entered the crisis window, the transition phase – that heroic journey into the underworld – where we will be forced to experience a shamanic initiatory experience, perhaps a near-death experience, before we can emerge as an adolescent species with a new, more mature mind. Until we reach that stage, however, we will have to struggle with the death throes of the old mind, as old systems cling to power and global infrastructures attempt to remain in control of a world in transition...the 'dark passage' that we are now venturing into. This is part of our collective *rites of passage*: it will shake us, reshuffle and reorientate a great deal of life on the planet; and it will also, hopefully, catalyse and prepare us for a psychophysical transformation. The reorientation required – both psychological and physical – may be far from linear...as we wrestle with the cloak of the old world system that clings onto a *modus operandi*, refusing to let go without a fight. Despite our glorious, gleaming, polished achievements that the world displays with pride, our current systems (social, cultural, political and economic) are remarkably anachronistic, cunningly deceptive, opaque, and in dire need of renovation. Yet in order to sweep out the brushwood we may be forced to endure a metaphorical, and literal, *dark night of the soul*. The next 20 years cannot be the same as the last 20 years. Change is upon us rapidly, even if we are not aware of its pace.[20]

We were not aware of the pace as I wrote those words; and many are no more aware now even though that pace has dramatically quickened. At each cyclical renewal we are faced with prophecies of the 'End Time' that also throw up images and imaginations of the world apocalypse. Yet such an apocalypse is not a fatality but a revelation – a *revealing*. It marks the disintegration of one narrated cycle and the emergence of new mythological voices as heralding a departure from the dying throes of an aeon of time. At such a moment, the aftermath of an apocalypse/revealing lies a great expanse where reality itself requires a re-stitching together and reimagining. A new operation of *worlding* comes into being. There is a change of guard of the arch"itypes: the social-status figures of leaders, politicians, and bankers are replaced by the metaphysician, the mystic, and the prophet.[21]

It is said that the nearness of an end of an era brings with it a sense of otherworldliness. It is at such threshold moments where the veil thins to allow a penetration, a mergence, of energies from various

· · · · · · · · · · · ·

20 Taken from my book *New Revolutions for a Small Planet* (2012 – Watkins Books)

21 Campagna, Federico (2021) *Prophetic Culture: Recreation for Adolescents*. London: Bloomsbury Academic.

sources, physical and metaphysical. Dimensions start to crossover and intervene; boundaries begin to dissolve. It is then that the illusion of ordinary, consensus reality is fast breaking down; this very same illusion that shielded many people from infra-psychic incursions. According to philosopher Rene Guenon, the extremity of materialistic beliefs and practices leads to a 'solidification of the world,' and it is this solidification that causes 'fissures' to open up through which 'infra-psychic' forces enter. In other words, humanity is invaded by the specters of its own psyche. The reality of unknown psychic powers, and their influences, from beyond our world has always been part of human knowledge – only that now it comes out from its occult shell and more into visibility. The dissolution of the physical world, its fragmentation, chaos, and disarray, catalyzes the psychic manifestations that represent the phase of the dissolution of the present cycle. The dissolution of the present cycle of materialism only begets a necessary re-creation of the world. The hardening and extremity of corruption of our physical world must also lead to a degree of psychological fracturing if a new psycho-physical environment is to unfold. That is, unless there are cracks within the highly conditioned collective psychosphere of humanity, how can the light get it?

Every human soul is infused with a sense, a knowing, of the Transcendent – a filament or spark of Source – of the Alpha and Omega of all existence. Ignorance of it only exists on this physical, earthly plane, and obscured by the degraded forces of deep materialism.

The inner faculty which recognizes this is often referred to as the Heart, and is the human being's highest faculty – although it lies dormant or slumbering within most people. This is an incorruptible, inviolable element within the human – a 'supramental organ of knowledge' – that is beyond mind or intellect. The sense of the transcendent implies an inner urge, longing, or pull to transcend the limitations of this plane of reality. These urges are the signs of the times – the moment of the eleventh hour. The contact with Source energy is available (gives) to those who are aware of it: 'For unto every one that hath shall be given, and he shall have abundance: but from him that hath not shall be taken away even that which he hath.' (Matthew 25:29). It is at the eleventh hour, from a dissolution to a new beginning, that we understand also the phrase: 'and the last shall be first.'

Materialism & the Loss of Soul

The non-material, or non-visible, realm does not lie dormant. It is active, constantly. It is what infuses and makes possible the world we know and see. The intangible realm of vital forces is what we often call the 'spiritual' dimension for within it lies the conscious intelligences that establish material life. Spiritual matters have long been an abstract thing for many people. Yet they are no longer to remain abstract – they are now to flow into culture not only through so-called 'spiritual channels,' but through all manner of ways, including people. The flow and merger between the suprasensory world and the sensory world (the realm of the phenomenal), has always been in operation. Only now, it looks set to increase.

Materialism is all good and well – yet up to a certain point. This is recognized by some as the 'Fall' – the deep immersion into physical reality. To a certain degree, this immersion into physicality was necessary for developing individualism and to perceive existence in relation to Source. Once this recognition is gained, then begins the 'return journey' back to Source/Origin consciousness. However, if a species remains too long within the grip of materialistic forces, then a hardening – or *deadening* – can occur that crystallizes certain faculties and organs of perception, which leads to an evolutionary stagnation. As such, the stagnation of evolvement can be due to the over-influence of entropic forces. The impulse of spiritual knowledge (developmental forces) descending into the physical world has been opposed by other forces that do not wish for people to discover their inner freedom. Yet this time, this moment in human development, has been foreseen and, on some levels, even planned for. What is to come about has been viewed as inevitable by those who know what is at stake.

The entropic forces that exist in opposition aim to 'over-materialize' materialism. They intend to deepen the entanglement within physical matter, and to create artificial material forms that would not have arisen in the natural course of human evolvement. This is a matter of exercising certain powers upon the physical plane. This is being applied in such a way as to block a renewal of human culture beyond materialism and to direct it into a new form of materialism, a more etheric form that seems un-material. This is what I refer to as the 'fallacy of materialism' – the digital-virtual realms, whilst seeming contrary to physical-materialism, are in fact working to deepen human entanglement in material forces. These digitized spaces, because of their sense of non-physicality, are really an etheric manifestation of materialism. Or rather, a realm of theoretical materialism. Theoretical materialism signifies a reality construct that does not need to be physical to the touch, yet it is based on, or is a projection from, a material foundation. Within both the theoretical and regular mode of materialism, the human being is encapsulated within an amalgamation of material processes. It is also a world of facts and external evidence that a person becomes lost within. All life experience proceeds from this material realm, and this conditions the human being to gain a view of life that is factually based, and to accept that there is no other reality except this world of materialism and factual experience. Any notion of the soul or spirit – the transcendental impulse – is either regarded as being a by-product from material reality or is rejected altogether as a false notion. This is the power of the immersion into matter-reality.

Deep materialism finally becomes a cosmology of entropy and decline. It leads to mechanical, artificial modes of thinking that eventually brings about a stagnation in those forces driving human development. If continued, these materialistic forces carve out a path of technological advancement and evolution that further blocks vital, spiritualized forces. In this route, the human being strives

74

for greater material benefits yet neglects the vital human forces of spiritualized connection. Our current epoch is concerned with the development of the material world; and if the human being is not to degenerate totally into a mere accomplice of machines, then a path must be found which leads from the mechanical impulse towards a life of the spirit. However, entropic forces are in play that are opposed to forms of spiritualization (spiritual freedom), and which work to reduce and, eventually, dispose of spiritual seeking and to replace it with an ethereal and otherworldly 'virtual paradise' where all needs can be fulfilled-by-illusion. A part of this 'supra-materialism' is the notion of immortality that is arising through transhumanist tropes. This can be referred to as the *immortality falsehood* as it works not through the spirit-soul but through a prolongation of the physical life experience by merger with machinic forms. This is a mode of potential immortality within the physical sphere but not within the spiritual. In the end, it is an entrapment for it disavows the inner spirit release from the physical domain. This can lead to a state of soullessness within the human being as the contact with Source becomes, over time, diminished. Or, perhaps this materialistic, transhumanist agenda will attract those people already without full spirit-soul incarnation.

It may be that there are people walking around in physical incarnation, in physical bodies, yet who are lacking, for want of a better word, a *soul*. Rudolf Steiner made note of this a hundred years ago when he stated

'...a kind of surplus of individuals is appearing in our times who are without Egos ['I'], who are not truly human beings. This is a terrible truth...They make the impression of a human being if we do not look closely, but they are not human in the fullest sense of the word.' [1]

Steiner warned us to be aware that what we encounter as human beings in human form may not always have to be what it appears to be. He stated that the outer appearance can be just that: appearance. He went on to state: 'We encounter people in human form who only in their outer appearance are individuals...in truth, these are humans with a physical, etheric, and astral body, but beings are embodied in them, beings that make use of these individuals in order to operate through them.'[2] What this refers to is that human bodies can be vessels for other beings to operate through.

This makes us realize that the world of 'spirit' may not always be what we have thought it to be. In other words, it may not be all divine light and ascension. It also involves the aspect of *discernment*. For there are players and forces that wield a great deal of influence within the physical world. And some of these influences act through the presence of certain individuals that may appear outwardly 'normal.' In this light, a completely different kind of spirituality is at work in present-day humanity. It may be inferred, without sounding dramatic, that certain power groups, and their important individual members, are influenced (and perhaps dominated) by a non-human species of being that are intent on implementing non-human objectives. Such groups and individuals would, in this case, exhibit a distinct lack of 'soul' – i.e., empathy and compassion – and would appear to others as displaying almost sociopathic tendencies.[22] Yet at the same time, such people can appear unusually charismatic and are able to exert great influence over other people, especially with their words and speeches, whilst being themselves emotionally stunted.

To consider this further, such beings might be motivated in their actions to attempt to block other human being's connection to their own individual inner/ spiritual impulse. By a range of actions, they could focus on distracting people away from the notion of a metaphysical reality and of their inherent connection to Source (or a realm of vital conscious intelligence beyond matter-reality). In extreme cases, such players might even target the bio-psycho human body in an attempt to sabotage the vessel so as to make it a less viable vehicle for soul-spirit incarnation. What else might they hope to achieve? Again, referring to Rudolf Steiner, he stated that:

> 'Their objective is to maintain the whole of
> life as a mere economic life, to gradually
> eradicate everything else that is part of the

· · · · · · · · · · · ·

22 Or refer to Jon Ronson's book *Th Psychopath Test* (2012)

intellectual and spiritual life, to eradicate the spiritual life precisely where it is most active...and swallow up everything through the economic life.'[3]

By hijacking cultural, social, and economic systems, the focus turns away from the inner life, which tends to be more active once people have satisfied their primary needs. Also, if there are uncertainties, disruptions, and fluctuations in these systems, then people can become psychologically influenced in a negative way. That is, for those people who come under the domination of such economic forces – i.e., are subservient through debt – they are more likely to experience a loss of personal empowerment and will. If we take only a cursory glance at the actions of many incumbent leaders, politicians, corporate businesses, financial institutions, and more, we can see a clear lack of any soulful behaviour or intent. Quite the contrary, many of these individuals and groups seem determined to curtail human freedoms, sovereignty, and inner empowerment. If Steiner were alive today, he would no doubt say that what we are currently witnessing upon the physical plane is an act of soulless terraforming of the planet and a controlling manipulation of the human life experience by nefarious forces that have anti-human aims and intentions. Perhaps this is why so many people today are experiencing depression, frustration, and apathy – a paralysis of will – from which they feel unable to resolve. This gets manifested as a sense of weariness and dissatisfaction that is projected out into their everyday lives.

Because of this, and other factors, the consciously aware person of today is being asked to step into their role as a physical representative of sacred life. It is important that metaphysical realities are never diminished or disowned, and that the life of the spirit remains healthy and strong in expression within physical life. If there is ever a struggle against the human soul, then we may be witnessing this in these current times. We would do well to remember that each person possesses that *special treasure* that can never be taken from them. And this is the true eternal and genuine immortality. These are the times to be soulful, and to bring forth the human spirit.

References

[1] Cited in Grosse, Erdmuth Johannes (2021) *Are There People Without A Self?* Forest Row: Temple Lodge, p31-2

[2] Cited in Grosse, Erdmuth Johannes (2021) *Are There People Without A Self?* Forest Row: Temple Lodge, p60

[3] Cited in Grosse, Erdmuth Johannes (2021) *Are There People Without A Self?* Forest Row: Temple Lodge, p63

The Soul of Today:
The Spirit as the Sign of the Times

*If we do not develop within ourselves this deeply rooted feeling
that there is something higher than ourselves, we shall never
find the strength to evolve to something higher.*

Rudolf Steiner

Humanity is passing through a difficult phase in its
development, and of concern is the potential risk of being
plunged into deeper states of materialism and automatism.
These two states are often in cooperation together, for the
deeper we become embedded in material forces then the
greater are the influences that can make us act without
conscious thought or intention. It can also be said that there
are certain forces, or agents, in this current time that are
pushing for greater immersion into materialism in order
to paralyze or prevent humanity's spiritual development.
In this regard, even the notion of anything 'spiritual' has
come to be either ridiculed, diluted into commercialism,
or hijacked into pseudo-spiritual forms (such as corporate
retreats and online guruism). It is important that we now
cast a critical eye upon the state of human society and the

nature of our times. This is not to criticize but to draw attention – to be aware of its aspects – as if to shine a light upon it. It is necessary to look beyond the 'scenery of external affairs.'

For those people caught up within the external civilization of the moment, with its impacts, distractions, and stimulations, it is difficult to acknowledge the existence of knowledge and perceptual understanding that lies beyond the conditioned senses. Yet it must also be said that now is the time for people to live, and be guided, more in accordance with inner, or esoteric, principles than ever before. It is this connection with one's inner life that brings greater awareness onto external events. And without this awareness, this degree of perceptive insight, then we allow greater concentrations of power to be wielded in the hands of the few, who will exercise this control over the masses in a negative way. What is necessary is awareness and intention emerging through each individualized person. It is this state of individualization, as opposed to group/mass behaviour, that marks the correct stage of human development for these times.

Taking the work of Austrian thinker/mystic Rudolf Steiner, the state of human perception and awareness can be recognized as relating to three soul stages: sentient, intellect-mind, and consciousness. Within the stage of sentient soul (i), the human being lives primarily within the world of the senses. They are drawn into their passions, desires, and are easily manoeuvred or manipulated into following trends, politics, and mass movements. These people form the majority, are swayed by the media, and are the general masses that move with the machinations of the mob. They are influenced by the 'influencers,' convinced by the consensus narrative, and swim in the mainstream. The second stage, that of the intellect-mind soul (ii), represents the person of the intellect who strives to free themselves from the rash impulses of the senses. They are aware of these tendencies yet steer themselves by rational thinking. They also attempt to keep their feelings under check and express their heart's desire through critical engagement. At the same time, this rational ordering often allies such people with conservatism, dogma, ideologies and a sense of righteousness. As they can manipulate others, so too can they be manipulated by their own allegiance to fixed systems. They can be blinded by ideals and uncritical of their own weaknesses. Such people can appear exceedingly clever whilst lacking humanity. Broadly speaking, such people fill the ranks of the political and leadership organizations. And the third stage, that of the consciousness soul (iii) has yet to fully emerge within the current epoch. It is this stage that deals with the formation of the aware individual who is not easily influenced or swayed by the emotional-psychological masses, and the strategies employed for these persuasions.

The phase of individualization within humankind was, and continues to be, a necessary step to release the human being from the previous mode of group consciousness. The egoistic self was required in this transference into individualization. Yet the danger now is that this operational ego grows beyond its function and becomes a dominant aspect of the human being. Acting and striving from the egoistic self is what leads to the imbalance and inequality of the world. The stage of individualization is bound up with increased egoism, yet this is a necessary relationship to reach the depths of self-realization. It becomes troublesome when the ego, instead of leading to inner growth, gets projected externally and becomes the major aspect of the outward personality. This can lead to stunted inner growth and continued external ego projection. The extremity of this is when a person sinks back into group consciousness and seeks security within a group environment. This can lead to cultic tendencies, as well as nationalism and other ideological and religious groupings. Part of the polarity tension in world affairs has been the pull between the dominant egoists and the group mentality masses. However, it can also be recognized that this stage of growth has to be lived and experienced in order to be moved through. The strains and stresses increase when people seem incapable, or are disallowed, from moving beyond this stage of human development. In this case, the person remains at the level of the lower 'I', which is a mass phenomenon and below that of full individualization. The lower self becomes the dominant expression of the personality, and this can literally run amok, getting entangled in passions, persuasions, disagreements, and disputes. The worst case of affairs is when societies establish structures, systems, and forms of management that cater to this lower stage of human development. People are then caught in a loop, where the base behaviours of this lower individualization are sustained and supported, deliberately creating a civilization of stagnation and stunted growth. The task here is for people to take the direction of their life into their own hands.

The human being must establish an intention to develop their aligned individualization for it seems that there are forces opposed to this human evolvement. For this reason, it is now essential that a perceptive state of consciousness (referred to in Steiner terminology as the consciousness soul) is allowed to emerge among those people receptive and prepared for this. The consciousness soul can be said to elicit higher morals and values within the individual. This requires also that the person has an inner freedom and the ability to perceive and act beyond the confines of social conditioning. This is a form of perceptual thinking as opposed to programmed thinking. The human being has it in their power to transform themselves whilst participating in active life. In fact, life provides friction for the transformational process. And this transformation takes place in the innermost self, which later can be projected outwards into life. It is not enough to affect correct behaviour if the inner life is stunted (as is the case with so many people, especially those most visible upon the world stage). As Rudolf Steiner put it:

'For every human being bears a higher man within himself besides what we may call the work-a-day man. This higher man remains hidden until he is awakened. And each human being can himself alone awaken this higher being within himself. As long as this higher being is not awakened, the higher faculties slumbering in every human being, and leading to supersensible knowledge, will remain concealed.'[23]

Steiner also considered entropic forces (what some would call 'evil' or de-evolutionary forces) as a necessary part of human development. Such forces create the friction that fuels potential development, such as the friction between the road and the tyre helps create the movement of the car. To a degree, such forces are unavoidable in physical existence. All development is a matter of stages, and each stage must be reached before attempting the move to another. Where is humanity at this current scale of development, we may wonder?

Each person must decide for themselves how they wish to live life. It can be said that a person who is ignorant of this decision, or who negates making such a decision, is more likely to fall under the sway of entropic

. . . .

23 Rudolf Steiner, *Knowledge of the Higher Worlds* (1947 English translation by George Metaxa)

forces, for it is these forces that target/attract the unaware or lazy souls. This recognition should encourage us to make perceptive choices in life. In every sphere of human life – whether social, cultural, or political – there are forces in operation that represent spheres of activity of greater magnitude than most people are able to realize. There are 'universal forces' that have been in contention – in motion – for a very long time. As for human beings, all motion, all movement, requires effort. That the many are unaware of this, only places more emphasis upon the responsibility of the few who are aware. This has always been the case and is likely to remain so for the time ahead. The inner impulse towards working for the greater good of humanity – the 'macrocosmic good' – comes out of genuine understanding and not general emotions or mass psychology. It is also the responsibility for such aware individuals to gain an understanding, a level of perspective, for perceiving the events of our time. It is this understanding of forces behind events at face value that helps in the growth of the consciousness soul. Just as we can recognize there are occult forces in play in the physical realm, so too does this suggest that there are forces operable beyond the physical domain. To not acknowledge this is the same as seeing the branches of a tree swaying in the wind and to consider that the branches are moving of their own accord and under their own volition. It is a fundamental error to mistake secondary phenomena for primary causes. And when a person acts out of limited understanding, there is the potential to serve not the good but ultimately the contrary. In terms of entropic forces (my term for 'evil'), they cannot be banished for they form a part of existence; rather, they are to be *transmuted into good* for them to be overcome. And this is the task of our times, the task for the spiritual soul of today.

What is needed is a re-cognition and refocusing upon metaphysical realities. Rudolf Steiner stated that if all human beings were to decide that they did not want higher development, then this potential for development would come to an end. It is therefore the responsibility of those with awareness, and inner cognition, to maintain within humankind the urge for inner evolvement. The present task for responsibly aware people today is to seek out that knowledge which comprehends not only world forces but the primary causes of events in this phenomenal, physical realm. In doing so, the person is able to raise themselves beyond petty inclinations and selfish, egoistic behaviour. This is not a denial of physical reality but rather a strengthened recognition of the primary realm of spirit.

To conclude, it can be said that there are forces coming through into this realm that humanity has no previous knowledge or experience of. This is not something to be afraid of, for these forces are a part of humanity itself. We-You-I are part of the same consciousness, only that material existence – the physical life – has split, divided, and splintered these aspects. Humanity, for the most part in recent times, has been living as if a partial existence – a semi-existence – for it has been cut-off from recognition of its Source and the greater field of consciousness. The planet Earth, as well as other planets in the solar system, are entering a new alignment where it shall be easier for these correspondences to be made. That this age was coming has been known for a long time by other groupings that have power and influence within human civilization. For this reason, these groupings have come together to create conditions across the planet – physical, mental, psychical – that would attempt to halt the emergence of greater perceptive consciousness. The attempts being made across the planet are for the realization of anesthetizing certain aspects of the human being so that it is less receptive to 'spiritual' or metaphysical truths and their correspondences. In other words, humanity is being further cut-off from its inherent connection to developmental impulses. Yet this approach has only a limited range of success. Humanity's faculties can only be 'blinded' for so long. Evolutionary, developmental forces are far more powerful than supposed by these planetary power groups. At the same time, we need to recognize that events of world history are symptoms of the occurrences on the metaphysical level of reality, where primary, non-material aspects have their existence. These essential, primary phenomena have their impulses that come into being within the physical world of secondary phenomena. For most of humankind, these primary aspects are the *unknowables*.

It is time to become receptive to the forces available

to us so that as a human being we can be of assistance rather than ignorant or, worse still, a hindrance. For those people capable of developing their understanding and receptivity to such impulses, it is time to begin the journey to know of the unknowables.

Revival or Reckoning:
Allowing for Future Pathways

'Humanity needs to take up that which flows down from the spiritual heights into earthly life. It can be rejected. If it is rejected there then ceases for those people who have rejected it the possibility of human progress, of cultural progress, of human civilization, and the further development of humanity will have to be sought among other peoples, and in other areas...'

Rudolf Steiner

A revelation, or renewal, of the inner life of the human being is now of paramount importance. This is the window of time, of opportunity, as humanity finds itself fraught with uncertainties and many unwelcome forces. What is required is nothing less than a human re-evolutionary revival from lower impulses and stunted understanding towards a fuller realization of self. This is time for a 'reckoning' with oneself, for there to be any chance of developing our innate human higher faculties. This is not a time for drawing back and retreating into one's inner cave of darkness and ignorance, like an individualized expression of the medieval ages. Collective ignorance was a state that had to be passed through for there to be a stepping into an individualized self-awareness. A period of 'inner sleeping' has enabled humanity to be in a position to regain its spirit-consciousness faculties as if anew. And abstract truths were dominant so as to force people to reach forth for more recognizable inner truths. Modernity was arrived at through this period of gradual individual awakening from a slumber of mass formation, or mass conditioned mentality. To remain at this level would be disastrous for human development, for it would indicate a falling back into lower states of vibration based upon base instincts and appetites. It would also lead to opening the door towards further, and much increased, domination and enslavement. What is needed is for a significant number of individuals to recognize the inner tools and capacities they already possess, and to relate to these.

What this entails is not to get caught up, entangled, in the narrative of existing as singular beings adrift in a world populated by other singular beings, cut-off from meaningful and resonant connections. The human being is a relational creature; that is, we are constantly in correspondence, and communication, with an abundance of life external to us. And yet the mainstream narratives of psychological conditioning are compelling people to 'protect rather than connect.' This is not a time for closing down but of opening up. There have been preparations made for this time; the human being has been rewired so that resonant syncing will fall into place. Yet this can be blocked if people close down their receptors through fear, anguish, anxiety, and so on. These external fear stimulants have been deliberately unleashed for this purpose of closing people down to their innate inner facilities and abilities. The point here now is to *allow more* rather than shutting out. The over-abundance of external stimulus – misinformation, media dissonance, extreme visuals, scare-mongering, etc., – all work to interfere with a person's own relation to self. And the immediate response to this can often be to close up into a selfish mode of anxiety and anger.

The grasping onto one's anxiety raises the spectre of protectionism and pity; and this state suggests an acceptance that one may be wounded. And to be wounded also is suggestable of being in 'victim mode.' This immediately shifts a person into a lower vibratory state. Also, this state of mind/being causes a person's vital forces to contract, pull in, and close off. A person then becomes an island unto themselves. Paradoxically, the need to 'belong,' when one is in this state, is not relational – i.e., reaching out to specific contacts or friends – but rather mass-minded. In other words, a 'wounded person' seeks solidarity and comfort within the security of the masses. And this also entails accepting the mass narrative consensus, along with the 'security' of the authoritative body (e.g., the state) that supports and maintains this mass minded dominant narrative. The reckoning of self accordingly calls for a readjustment to self. This readjustment is, in my view, an allowance – a receptivity – to the developmental impulse that is flowing into physical life from without. As Austrian mystic

Rudolf Steiner stated in the opening citation, humanity now needs to take up that which is flowing 'down from the spiritual heights into earthly life.' It can be rejected, he notes; yet if it is rejected then there is the consequence that those people who have rejected it lose the possibility for their further development. And in this, they also hinder the progress of human civilization as a whole. This may sound dramatic, yet we need also to recognize what is at stake in these times.

The more we close ourselves off – to protect and disconnect – the more we are in danger of calibrating our lives in alignment to a machinic character. That is, to a mode of automation. This then clears the path towards transhumanism and the domination of technocratic impulses. A closed-down person is the ideal candidate for inclusion into a socially managed and mind-programmed mass. This must be seen now for these forces and impulses are arriving with increasing speed and ferocity. This is a *transitioning point* for humanity, for at this point comes the moment of choosing a particular developmental path for the species. It is imperative that we do not get caught up within a mesh of materialism that supplies many fantasies and promises, yet ultimately delivers a package of containment and control. Instead, we can align ourselves from a differing point of place, for this is indeed our right as sovereign individuals.

The impact and consequences of the incoming forces and impulses very much depends upon the state of consciousness with which they are met. And this will determine how humanity progresses, and whether it develops in evolutionary alignment or not. Certain forces, both those operating within visibility and those non-visibly, would prefer that humanity resides in a state of unknowing. To this end, it is our present responsibility to strive to be more and more conscious, and to stimulate conscious awareness in as many people as possible. It is no longer a long-term feasibility to remain in ignorance of the aims behind world affairs, or the processes that target people's beliefs and thinking patterns. Similarly, to be absent of the transcendental impulse in our lives is ultimately a path to stagnation in terms of inner development. As a species, we either evolve and develop, or we do not. And the evolvement of the human species entails that we become receptive to, and aware of, the cosmic impulses that connect us to Source consciousness. This knowledge needs to become more generally known and spoken about, rather than kept occult as it has been for ages past. Otherwise, the human species is in danger of succumbing to entropic influences that will work to diminish critical thinking, imaginative expression, and freedom of the life experience.

The increasing role of machinic logic, of cleverness, now being praised and encouraged is a different path to that of genuine wisdom. As the elusive Japanese sage Setsuna once said: *'It is not wise to be clever.'* The more people that can meet their external influences consciously, the more realization will be gained. The outer trend of these times is deceit. Deceit in our once-trusted institutions; in our socio-cultural systems; in our bodies of information, education, and entertainment. These are none other than forces of decay rather than development; and they represent the withering rather than the blooming of the seed. Such entropic forces are the forces of opposition regarding the spiritual advancement of humankind. And these forces have been compelled to make their move now, before enough individuals within the collective gain conscious awareness and recognize the reality of the transcendental impulses that connect humanity with Source. This is the period of spirit-consciousness, which is why the counterforces are working desperately to act against these developmental processes. It is in this period that the conscious, individualized, independent thinking human being is required to emerge. It is the moment for revelation – a human revival – or our reckoning.

A period such as we are facing now calls for dedication and commitment; for if not, then the encroaching impulses of apathy and impotence will serve to diminish the human being's receptive capacities. And these receptive capacities are required for the conscious receiving of transcendent impulses – otherwise they will be turned into mechanical, materialistic efforts. Independent, self-willed perceptive thought (which includes the heart resonance) is necessary for regaining the intuitive insight that once was natural to the human being. Humanity is poised upon this path of potential advancement; only to be hindered by forces that deliberately aim to hold us back. The choice here is to remain dumbed and numbed – that is, psychologically mummified – by the mainstream mind-programming of the dominant consensus reality, or to work quietly and persistently with our personal efforts. Through self-discipline and focused awareness, each person can work to develop their own forms of heightened perception. And this begins by claiming one's self-identity before it is lost amidst a cultural confusion of manufactured identities and deliberate 'politically correct' fluidities.

The decision here is between aligning oneself with those developmental forces that seek to bring humanity into a merger with Source consciousness; or the entropic forces that push for selfish, egoistic domination. This is the distinction between choosing from cleverness or wisdom. The present work for the human being – here and now – I would say, is the acceptance of, and receptivity to, what is called the 'Spirit' (Source consciousness), and to facilitate its emergence through the material realm. The human being can act as the transformative force in the material world by being *in the world* whilst simultaneously *transcending* it.

Unconscious Becoming Conscious: understanding the nature of negative forces

'What people of the fifth post-Atlantean epoch must learn to recognise is the fully conscious struggle against the evil rising up in the evolution of humanity.'

Rudolf Steiner, 18 November 1917

According to Austrian metaphysician Rudolf Steiner, the task of humanity in this epoch is to comprehend the relation of good and evil; especially, the human choice between good and evil, and the challenge of evil to make humanity more aware of spirit-consciousness. In our present age, we are to experience the negative counterforces in order to move through to greater development. Steiner stated that the 'forces of evil' exist in the world so that humanity might, at the appropriate time, break through into a 'life of the spirit.'[24] The presence of the counterforces gives humanity an opportunity to gain insight into the human condition, as well as the life conditions in this earthly domain. By having some understanding of the intention of opposing forces, a person is better prepared for continuing their own

• • • • • • • • • • • •

24 Mentioned in a lecture given on 26th October 1918 (GA 185)

journey. That is, we each can learn from our encounters with negating forces; we can take these encounters as an opportunity to connect more strongly with our own force of will. In the words of philosopher Sergei O. Prokofieff:

> In addition to working intensely on oneself, especially with regard to eradicating falsehood of any kind and all aspects of fear, together with all overt and secret inclinations towards materialism – something different is required, namely, a working together of human beings in the social realm that is based on spiritual principles.[25]

In advocating the coming together of spiritually minded people, it is not our responsibility to be concerned with those who Steiner called the 'soulless' ones. Rather than being pulled into the influence of such people (with their lower vibrational energies), it is more beneficial for a person to transform their immediate environment into a more harmonious energy. Another way of saying this is that the presence of negativity is to be transmuted into that which is not negative or counterproductive. This is akin to an alchemical procedure.

· · · · · · · · · · · · ·

25 Sergei O. Prokofieff, *The Encounter with Evil* (Temple Lodge, 2001), p62

The 21st century is a transformatory epoch, where we shall have to face our shadows and deal with them. Without this acknowledgement, and cleansing, we will be dominated by the forces of stagnation. Later, when this catharsis or 'cleansing' has been achieved, we may collectively move into a stage of *transmutation* where the negative is transmuted into constructive forces. The spirit of our times, therefore, is one of transmutation and transformation. And until counterforces are transmuted, there is no real or lasting transformation. This 'transmutation of the negative/shadow' is the leitmotif of our epoch, and it cannot be done without passing through 'the valley of the shadow of death;'[26] experiencing and, above all, understanding both the forces of negation and those of development. As author Terry Broadman writes:

> In saying that, we immediately meet a paradox, because we need to recognise that without the resistance posed to our development by these counterforces, there would be no human freedom possible and therefore, ultimately no possibility for love either. No great drama, especially the great drama of the story of mankind, is possible without the challenge from forces of darkness within us.[27]

. . . .

26 A phrase relating to a version of Psalm 23 in the King James Bible.
27 http://threeman.org/?p=3040

By casting light upon those forces that oppose human freedom, we may also see that, somewhat paradoxically, it is these same forces that make freedom possible. And yet, we need to gain this realization so we can know what we are up against.

Entropic counterforces attempt to control and manage human thinking and cultural narratives through arid materialism – the forces of limitation, indifference, rational logic, and consumption, for example. Such arid forces seek to constrain and contain human thinking by limiting it to the physical domain. That is, by negation and denial of the metaphysical background to life; a worldview that recognises no spirit-consciousness or genuine inspiration from beyond the material realm. It can be said that such counter-evolutionary forces wish to ensure that humanity remains at the level of the 'lower ego;' that is, our base level 'everyday' selves, ruled by passions, possessions, promises, and pseudo-truths. We have already seen how modern life is rife with the self-centred materialist concerned only for their physical pleasures and gains. This is the false-polished underbelly of a capitalist-fed globalist agenda. This is the sphere where the tightly controlled culture industry provides ultimate dissonance through glamour-distraction. Cacophonous music, jarring rhythms, and discordant lyrics appeal to the basest impulses within the tranced modern listener. It is little wonder then that there is resistance to those people who wish to develop their inner senses and modes of perception. The everyday environment is not conducive to the development of spirit-consciousness. And yet, it is the role of awakened individuals to assist the unconscious in becoming conscious.

Entropic forces can be regarded as *forces of hindrance*. For various reasons, they have not fulfilled their developmental potentials; they have faltered in their path, and thus 'fallen by the wayside.' And as wayside creatures, they hinder and disrupt all other wanderers and walkers upon the path. It can be said that they belong to our realm but are no longer upon our developmental path. Such counterforces are not creative; that is, they are not a creative principle in the universe, and so they need to make use of – or usurp – existing impulses to be able to act in the physical world. Such forces operate by distorting, and demonising, other processes and/ or vessels in order to function. We need to be aware of those beliefs, idealisms, organizations, groupings, etc, that show a deliberate antipathy and hostility towards aspects of spirit-consciousness and the metaphysical. These may be collective, and/or concealed, forces aiming to divert humanity's path of growth. The materialistic route is a caricature of what now needs to be the human being's present state. Total materialization, including the digital-virtual domains (such as the Metaverse) represent a paralysis of growth in spirit-consciousness. A total materialization of human consciousness is taking place across the world and is especially dominant within the technologically advanced nations.

Modern life has been turned upon itself to become a parody. Nothing can be taken at face value for the outer expressions have become corrupted. Pseudo-truths are the caricature of relative truths; deep fakes are the travesty of genuine selves; and the lines between knowing and unknowing have been deliberately smeared. The outer life, on its own, exists as a tarnished kingdom. The only thing to do is to extract oneself from this polluting sphere and to re-wire one's alignments, attachments, and allegiances. In previous epochs, the human being's inner authority was undermined by subjugating it to exterior bodies of authority – such as institutionalized religions. When the masses moved out of illiteracy and became educated enough to read, research, and learn for themselves, the exterior forms of authority shifted from the sacred to the secular. Secular institutions came to regulate social norms, thinking patterns, and modes of accepted behaviour. In present times, as conscious awareness and perceptive understanding expands rapidly, the exterior bodies of authority are attempting to gain leverage by gaining interior access to our bodies and minds – what I have referred to as the new forms of biopower. These interventions into the physical integrity of the human being have serious consequences for the natural expression of spirit-consciousness. If the human vessel is unbalanced, or bio-chemically – or even genetically – interfered with, then the incarnated spirit-consciousness will have trouble in manifesting within the physical.

This intervention can be taken to the extreme through advancements in the biological-genetic sciences. The process of human cloning is a further step in this domain. If a physical body is cloned, then it is basically manufactured – it has not been brought into life through an organic birthing process (regardless of how the fertilized egg was delivered into the female body). In a metaphysical sense, it can be said that the physical body is not capable of receiving spirit-consciousness for it is not vibrationally aligned. It is an empty vessel, in a spiritual sense. From this, it may be inferred that other entities or forces could inhabit such a physical vessel. Why is human science increasingly moving towards the automation, the techno-hybrid, the slicing and dicing with DNA and human genetics? In this, there is a shift toward splintering the human being from its metaphysical origins and from the domain of spirit. If anything, this is the definition of evil – the isolation of the physical from its metaphysical source.

The counter-developmental forces are acting against the human mind (psyche), the heart (emotions), and the body (will). These three aspects can be related to imagination, inspiration, and intuition. And these three aspects have been targets for manipulation for quite some time. In our current age, the imagination is targeted through the media, video games, propaganda, digital life, and augmented reality, for example. The faculties of inspiration are being distorted through a controlled culture-industry (music, literature, art). And the intuition is deadened through a weakening of the human will as well as interventions and violations against the physical body. All these forces aim to press down upon the human being in a way that increases its immersion in materiality whilst bringing forth more animalistic, or primitive drives. How much more difficult it is for spirit-consciousness to come into a life experience, only to find that everything is subordinated to a material perspective – a world that is almost oblivious to the reality of the spirit.

The more a person comes under the powers of this world, under the laws set within this materiality, the less a person can act from an inner place of personal and spiritual will. A human being can no longer truly become their essential self if they are wholly invested in a consensus reality that is averse to metaphysical truths. As Christ famously stated: 'My Kingdom is not of this world.' (John 18:36) Although not *of this world*, it must *work in this world*. Our point of interaction – participation and action – are within this world, yet our foundation does not originate from within this world. And this combination, this merger, is what creates a strength to be in this world and not to be worn down by it. The expression of spirit-consciousness is a *fusion* – and the human being is the vessel (the receptor as well as the carrier). Being the carrier for that which is also *beyond* the physical means also that the person needs to strengthen their interior world – their inner environment. A fully exteriorized person is too much attached with events and influences of the material world, and this can become a hindrance. There needs to be enough capacity within each person to exercise internal creative imaginations so that *received inspirations* have a vessel, a protected space, in which to gestate before outward expression. A 'new world' can come into being, yet it must come through the human being and not to be forced upon it. This is why it is said that a new world is *birthed* rather than built. The outer actions may be that of building, yet the initial impulses are birthed from within. It is in this way that metaphysical influences can enter into the domain of the physical – *through receptive individuals.*

The act of transmuting counteractive forces into constructive ones requires that humanity shifts from a place of outward dominance, under the sway of external influences, and into spaces of inward receptivity to inspirational impulses. In this, it can be said that the transformative process is one of the unconscious becoming conscious.

The Realm of Caesar & The Realm of Spirit

It is time to consider how to cultivate a *right relation* to the things of this world. That is, we should recognize that there are conditions specific to our physical existence – to matter-reality – that may not need apply to our existence as a human being *if* we can cultivate a particular inner state and relation to that which exists beyond physical reality. As Jesus is quoted as saying: 'Render unto Caesar the things that are Caesar's, and unto God the things that are God's.'(Matthew 22:21) There are those relations that exist (and often 'must' exist) with the outer physical world – we can call this the realm of Caesar. And there is the connection that a person can cultivate in relation to that which is beyond the physical – what we can broadly call the realm of spirit, or the transcendental impulse. There has been a growing tendency in outer life to deny the existence of anything beyond the physical. In Western society especially, even the talk of 'life after death' is received with sniggers and smirks and is rejected by the mainstream consensus thinking. In this sense, human society has degenerated in its perceptive understanding. In terms of metaphysical comprehension, we have become as little children. We are conditioned to laugh at tales of ghosts; we scoff when we hear of UFOs; we grin when hearing of so-called 'near death experiences' (NDEs) out-of-the-body. The list goes on and on. The fact of the matter is that external conditions have made it so that there is no respect or recognition for the truth – and very few people make an effort for expanding their perceptive understanding. The outer garb of our lives has usurped aspects of fundamental understanding and replaced them with superficial substitutions: power, celebrity, wealth, and the rest. Or worse, aspects of modern ideological dogma – the new 'wokism' – infiltrates our attention, and conditions our capacity to truly express ourselves. In such circumstances, a falsehood of existence is permitted where such substitution is considered not evil but, on the contrary, as the new social good. As Russian philosopher Nicolas Berdyaev put it: 'Falsehood is affirmed as some holy duty for the sake of higher purposes.'[1] It is the human condition today that what goes by the name of 'consciousness' is a structure of thinking and belief that has been adapted to the conditions of an artificial reality and delivered to the consumer (the individual). And we need to recognize that the average person interprets the world around them, and attributes meaning, through tainted lenses. As it is said: Everything that pours from a poisoned vessel must itself be tainted. It is the astute and aware individual who strives to make the distinction between that which belongs to the material world (Caesar) and that which relates to the metaphysical realm (the spirit). And it is a fallacy to 'think' that each individual lives in the same objective world. We do not: we each live within our subjective perceptual bubble that, in general, is outwardly steered by the dominant consensus narrative.

The human being is never quite 'normal.' There is no normality within this state of affairs. For this reason, many people find it difficult to attribute meaning to what they perceive as a meaningless world. And from the mass perspective, there is much within the world right now that appears maddeningly absurd. It seems that human life lives under no universal law and is only subjected to the local laws that govern the socio-economic life of each specific region. Freedom has come to mean the ability to access those desires and wishes that arise in us. It is a freedom that gives satisfaction whilst not questioning the perimeter that keeps us fenced into a life of restricted understanding. The general masses have been permitted to seek for their 'gods' through certain religious structural institutions yet are steered away from seeking genuine self-gnosis. We only have to look at the history of the Cathars (the so-called Albigensian heresy) to see an historical example of this. The denial of greater knowledge has been quite successful through the substitution in self-interest and the power-play of the Game of Life. Unless we have knowledge – real knowledge – to work upon ourselves, there is little hope of liberation from the servitude to a mechanized existence. We live in a time where the principal focus for progress is with the development of external techniques, hardly realizing that the more important work is to discover the techniques for changing oneself. The situation we are in is not only about the liberation of oneself from a life of automation; it is a question of how a changed person can live an effective outer life. We live in a world of disunity and hostility, of inequality and greed. Yet another condition of the world is possible, and it requires another type of knowing. A human being has always carried a deep secret within; it is the secret of belonging to an existence beyond the physical realm, and that the human being was born with the ability to overcome its earthly limitations and can access a greater understanding. But effort is required. As Berdyaev put it: 'Man's freedom lies in this, that beside the realm of Caesar there is also the realm of Spirit.'[2] It is the contestation between the 'realm of Caesar' and the 'realm of spirit' that can provide the impetus for discovering and refining our truer relations. In other words, it is the denying, negating forces that can act as catalysts to spur those active forces within us. The material world around us – the realm of Caesar – is a necessity for confirming to us that a means, a path, exists that can connect us to a realm beyond the physical. This gives us the outer confirmation that humanity exists under more than just physical-material conditions; that we are related to an order beyond that of our earthly existence.

This contestation between the realm of Caesar and the realm of spirit (the metaphysical realm) has been the cause for the continual historical clashes of power and the motivation for the drive towards totalitarianism. There has been a constant effort to diminish humanity's ties with the transcendental impulse and to cage the individual within a physical and perceptual prison. The race to technocracy is a race against humanity's development of increased cognition and perceptual awareness:

> 'The power of technics is the final metamorphosis of the realm of Caesar. It no longer demands the sanctification which the realm of Caesar demanded, in the past. This is the last phase of secularization, the dissolution of the centre and the development of various autonomous spheres, where one of them claims totalitarian recognition.'[3]

The current crises we are facing is a heightened manifestation of this historical clash of forces. There is a strong hand of physical organization and control that is ramping up the realm of Caesar into a modern machine of technique and automation. A new reality – an artificial one – is under construction, and it is going to be different from the past realities of organic or inorganic nature.[28] The new reality of Caesar is going to be merged into a digital apparatus, a civilization of machinic regulation and technique, which will distinguish itself from nature and carbon-based life. And along with this detachment from a carbon-based ecosystem will be a detachment from all things of the spirit-consciousness. The metaphysical realm will be banished and substituted by its avatar – the Metaverse. Future modern life will cease to be modern for it will have fallen back into a time where existence was devoid of a genuine centre of spirit. A time when through controlled information and education, people were conditioned to recognize the authority of the state as above and beyond all other law or order. We may be witnessing the emergence of a new Dark Age. Only that it will be a Dark Age dressed up in the Emperor's Clothes bought with shiny digital non-fungible tokens (NFTs).

With technique, or the modern 'smart technics, fast becoming the foundations of a 'new world order' we are witnessing a world moving into rationalized darkness. The whole process of life is becoming increasingly contradictory and absurd, only that this new order of rationalized technique is being sold as the 'new normal.' We shall soon be standing on our heads – and resisting calls to be turned the right way up. As one thinker put it: 'it is hard to agree to be turned upside down when one is

• • • • • • • • • • • •

28 See my book *Hijacking Reality: The Reprogramming & Reorganization of Human Life* (2021)

convinced that one is already the right way up.'[4] Through this upside-downness – this *inversion of life* – a new mode of authority is being granted to the realm of Caesar. The inner freedom of the human being is fast being eroded from without as the masses unknowingly succumb to a devastating psychic environment of manipulation and subtle (and also not-so-subtle) control. These modes of authority will seek to extend their power to become all-pervasive – these shall be the reign of the negating forces that the transcendental impulse will face in the coming years. The realm of Caesar shall become the Realm of Falsehood where 'good is realized by means of evil, truth by means of falsehood, beauty by means of ugliness, freedom by means of violence.'[5] The realization of inner truth, inner authority, does not come from the realm of Caesar directly; rather, it can be acquired only through the limitation of Caesar's realm. Caesar's realm may be a world which enslaves people through its deepening materialism; yet it also offers the potential for human evolvement through the very same negating forces. That which holds a person down can become the very same tools for their growth in awareness. After all, the visible world is a symbol of the world invisible. The unseen, or metaphysical realm, never forces itself upon us; yet its presence can be highlighted through its contradictory impulse.

A new birth is always preceded by contortions. A new seed must break through the upper crust of soil before it can grow further. Our task is not to focus upon

112

the resistance of the soil but upon the potential of the seed. That which slumbers shall awaken when the disturbance becomes too great to shrug off. A new birth is not an avenger against the old ways. As it is said: 'The avenger of past wrongs is not a new creature, he is still the old man.'[6] We cannot expect revolutionary resistance to produce the new human – yet a revolution in human affairs can produce the new human. And it is the new human who can reconnect to the realm of spirit and ensure that a denial of metaphysical reality is never again brought to bear within the realm of Caesar. And then, finally, we can hope to cultivate a *right relation* to the things of this world. And with a rightful heart and knowing conscience, we can say: 'Render unto Caesar the things that are Caesar's, and unto Source the things that are of the inner life.'

Notes

[1] Berdyaev, Nicolas. (1952) *The Realm of Spirit & The Realm of Caesar*. New York: Harper & Brothers, p13.

[2] Berdyaev, Nicolas. (1952) *The Realm of Spirit & The Realm of Caesar*. New York: Harper & Brothers, p41.

[3] Berdyaev, Nicolas. (1952) *The Realm of Spirit & The Realm of Caesar*. New York: Harper & Brothers, p48.

[4] Bennett, J.G. (1991) *What Are We Living For?* Santa Fe: New Mexico: Bennett Books, p18.

[5] Berdyaev, Nicolas. (1952) *The Realm of Spirit & The Realm of Caesar*. New York: Harper & Brothers, p94.

[6] Berdyaev, Nicolas. (1952) *The Realm of Spirit & The Realm of Caesar*. New York: Harper & Brothers, p166.

Life...in Reversal

'We must distinguish between real change and fictitious change. The change that comes from without, from externally imposed training and discipline, is fictitious...Real change comes from within, by conscious work intentionally performed by the being himself.'

J.G. Bennett

It is increasingly difficult in these times to speak of 'non-verifiable' or unprovable matters, especially concerns of the spirit-consciousness, for too many people are inculcated with fixed beliefs and thinking patterns. This is itself a sign of social conditioning and of a certain 'management of mind.' We should not be surprised that this situation is rife throughout our societies and cultures and is becoming increasingly predominant. Social norms are persuading many people to prefer safety and security rather than the potential discomfort that comes from gaining new realizations and understanding.

An ex-officer of the Soviet secret police who defected to the West (Gregory Klimov), revealed that in the fields of Soviet psychological warfare (and social psychology) they utilized the principles of psychoanalysis. In this, they saw the phenomena of evil as a 'complicated, complex social illness.' The psychoanalysts within the KGB equated evil with illness, especially an illness of the human psyche. This perspective places demonic actors and events as 'objective realities;' i.e., as various forms of illness of 'psyche and soul.' As the Russian anthroposophist G.A. Bondarev writes: 'The devils represents an *involved and complex process of degeneracy or retrogression that in the main consists of three parts: sexual deviation, psychic illnesses and some physical deformities of the organism.* The number of humans already afflicted with this degeneration is legion.'[1] Bondarev goes on to say that, based on certain social-psychological testing, the greatest degeneracy exists within the so-called elite of the world (as much as 75%). What this points to, concludes Bondarev, is a drastic decline of the human spirit. What it also tells us is that the phenomenon of 'evil' does not necessarily need to be personified or projected into certain personages *as it represents an illness of the human psyche.* We can recognize its presence operating within psychic imbalance and internal disconnect and detachment. And I would concur with Bondarev's conclusion in that such psychic dis-ease represents an inner disconnect with the transcendental impulse. This disconnect, or splintering, from a sacred source has now come to signify the nature of the *reversal* that epitomizes much of contemporary life.

It is within this reversal that we see much of the negating, or counter-evolutionary, forces within humanity.

116

And these forces have been dominating much of our everyday lives and continue to do so. I would suggest that it is our individual responsibility to recognize these forces, attempt to comprehend them, and to transform them into impulses that can work for humankind's evolvement. In this, we need to come to grips with the presence and activity of those aspects that signify a psychic illness, or dis-ease, within life. Such aspects are a feature of existence as much as positive, developmental forces. They all act within the playground of attraction, repulsion, and the expression of energy. The Rosicrucians recognized these forces when they referred to the *Deus Inversus* – or the 'Reversed God.' This nature of reversal works on humanity through the spheres of imbalance and disharmony to counteract civilizational development. The Austrian mystic Rudolf Steiner was aware of the future impact of such forces when he stated that: 'It is essential that the forces which manifest as evil if they appear at the wrong place must be taken in hand…in such a way that humanity can achieve something with these forces of evil that will be beneficial for the future of the whole of world evolution.'[2] In this regard, it is important that the individual becomes aware of the metaphysical realm that lies beyond the threshold of normal, or every day, consciousness.

If we remain unawares to our own forces of spirit-consciousness, then we are more susceptible to the manipulations of such counter-developmental forces. Those readers familiar with my writings will know that

117

I have attempted to draw attention to certain aspects of our consensus reality in order to gain greater clarity about how we may respond to the situation in a constructive way. I stand by what was written in the Gnostic Gospel of Philip: 'For so long as the root of wickedness is hidden, it is strong. But when it is recognized, it is dissolved. When it is revealed, it perishes.' Recognition, through heightened awareness and perception, brings more choice into play. The individual needs to be conscious of certain facts before they can manifest the correct intention and focus of will. What is needed is a culture of revelation – of 'uncovering' – rather than of cover up. It is through revelation that insight into the metaphysical foundation of life can be sustained within our increasingly materialistic societies. This access to metaphysical realities can never be wholly eradicated. Yet just a cursory glance at modern life indicates that there are attempts to deepen peoples' immersion into deteriorating forms of dissonance and distraction. This can be seen as a form of *reality deceit*.

Reality Deceit

The great deceit that is coming upon us is the unveiling of a so-called 'utopia' based on the isolation of the human spirit-consciousness. This fake promise is wrapped up in tech-salvationist terms, heralding a false ideal future. The real dis-ease of the human condition is to be in a state of estrangement. That is, estranged and alienated from any metaphysical influence or nourishment. It is not that the metaphysical background to life must necessarily be obvious to us, or tangible in our daily lives – only that we are cognizant of its existence and continual influence. Yet once this sense of recognition (the act of aware cognition) is dissolved, a barren soulless life is the result. And yet, in most circumstances, people will not be cognizant of this loss – this lack of the transcendental impulse in their lives – for they will be entrained into a reality consisting of a physical-digital mesh that keeps them attached to their lower nature and desires. This deceit consists of a most heinous form of enslavement, for it shall both be a willing one as well as an ignorant one. The splintering of the human being from its metaphysical connection shall go almost unnoticed, and the transfer into a reality of limited consciousness will have been enacted quite skillfully. This sly route to a human condition of alienation, procured through the guise of technological advancement and progress, will be a coup against the creative spirit. And this shall be the *reversal* of the human reality – the *reality deceit.*

The almost imperceptible dangers are that we have been slipping into a *reversed reality,* constructed through a realm of fantasy and make-believe, which now fuels the crass and superficial culture industries that dominate modern life. Any notion of Higher Reality has been twisted into an artificial lesser reality that attempts to hinder, as far as is possible, the developmental impulse from penetrating. This arrangement has culminated in dissociating humankind not only from its natural, organic, carbon-based environment, but also from an inherent contact with its origin – Source consciousness. This increasing disembodiment is reflected in such forms as the techno-digital ecosystem, extended reality (the Metaverse), computerization (including algorithms), and artificial intelligence. For many people today, their digital devices have become their instruments of salvation. But this salvation, this divine deliverance, belongs to the *Deus Inversus* – and we should choose our gods carefully. We should be careful too, not to be pulled into the encroaching banalization of life. And we should be on the look-out for signs and signals.

If anyone wishes to see how 'signals' can operate within the reality deceit, then watch all the episodes in the recent *Westworld* TV series (2016-2022). In Season Four, the machinic android 'hosts' have taken control of the world using a bioengineered virus that infects humans over the course of a generation, turning them docile and susceptible to AI and 'host' control. Storylines and narratives are created in order to give people their roles and characters in life, which they passively follow believing them to be their own life stories. Humankind is managed through these manufactured 'storylines' (a.k.a. socio-cultural narratives) that are transmitted directly to the minds and lives of humans through a series of radio-sonic transmission signals via the global technological infrastructure…But then again, this is just a fantasy story after all.

The course of external events that inform our political, economic, and cultural systems are not arbitrary, coincidental or natural. The modern human has been subtly manipulated into disconnecting from, and even shunning, the guidance of higher impulses. We are being told that the human being alone is the sole and dominant driving force for the future. And by this, we are propelled ever further into the personality construct with the human ego at the wheel. We are standing at the threshold of adopting a glorified materialistic view of life and the world. The spell of this disease is working to *over-materialize materialism* in a very deliberate and nefarious way. There may be some discomfort in the unfoldment of awareness, yet this is part of the transmutation of the disease.

Life 'in reversal' is working hard and fast on this intensifying of materialism. This deepening materialism not only denies the expansion of consciousness but is actively working to stagnate it. At the same time, we are moving through an impulse of increasing *individual awareness* against the backdrop of this over-materialization. Yet it is an awareness through the few, and not the many (yet). By recognizing that certain forces within the world are using processes of mass suggestion to introduce a simplification – or 'dumbing down' – of human consciousness, we can gain greater awareness over our condition and predicament. And in this awareness, we can gain a natural resistance and protection, as recognition allows a discernment to be made. It is this discernment to step away from the negating energies and frequencies of toxicity that can help a person to attune to a resonance of perceptive consciousness. By choosing where we place ourselves – our focus and attention – we can either take a step forward or stay where we are and stagnate. As always, the choice remains with us.

Notes

[1] Bondarev, G.A. (1993) *Crisis of Civilization* (2nd Edition). Printed by Wellspring Bookshop: London, p134

[2] Steiner, R. (2006) *Secret Brotherhoods and the Mystery of the Human Double*. Forest Row: Rudolf Steiner Press, p163

Moving Past the Threshold
(Understanding These Critical Times)

We are moving into significant times, and I feel it will be critical how we come to understand and perceive what is to come. How we frame the external 'happenings' that continue to erupt across the world will decide how we respond and cope with the effects. A few days ago, I posted a message on my Telegram channel. I wrote the following:

The more I observe external events unfolding, the more I perceive predictive programming at work. When we read or hear something in the mainstream media, we should understand that there is an intention to 'tell' us how things are – according to a set narrative. Mainstream narratives are programs, psychological manipulations, and often outright lies. We are given these narratives to program our beliefs. Our beliefs then create our perceptions, and our perceptions create our

123

experiences. Ultimately, we experience the world according to the narratives that we are given. This creates a loop – and many people remain in this 'perception loop.' In the coming days, weeks, and months, these loops are going to contain increasing dissonance, unease, and discomfort. We need to step away from them. We have to disentangle ourselves from the external programs and manufactured narratives. It is essential we step out of the lower frequencies of unrest and instability – and find our inner grounding. We can do better than this…

Why did I write this? Because I feel that the times ahead are going to be increasingly chaotic, and it is important that we do not get caught up in these disruptive energies. Everything external to us is calling for our attention and dragging our attention outwards and away from ourselves. And this not only makes us more attached to external events and occurrences, but also weakens our inner balance. Now is the time to be grounded and stable. And to *see clearly* that what are operating in the physical realm right now are only 'shadows.' They are the shadows of an older world, an older regime of power that is struggling with its last desperate breaths as a new revolution of understanding emerges. It is our time to acknowledge these struggles, without engaging with them, for they shall also allow us to gain our sovereignty, inner freedom, and comprehension of the bigger picture.

I haven't dipped into the Old Testament for decades (nor have I fully read it), yet this quote fell across my radar as I was writing this newsletter. In Ephesians 6:12 it was written that: "For our struggle is not against enemies of blood and flesh, but against the rulers, against the authorities, against the cosmic powers of this present darkness, against the spiritual forces of evil in the heavenly places"

The human struggle has been a long one, and continues to be so, for the path to perceptive awakening/awareness is not a daisy-strewn walk. Yet I feel that humanity is coming towards a threshold. A threshold in perception, awareness, understanding, and realization. And for this threshold to emerge, a pressure is building. I was speaking yesterday (22nd September) to my friend and colleague who receives the ABE messages (Nicola) about this feeling of energy. She immediately received a 'nudge' from ABE with the following communication:

> There's a pressure building up to push you pass the threshold. It will get your attention to enable you to look in a differing direction and not continuing in the same loop pattern now. It will be allowance on all levels now, for what had been a step-stall will now be step-relate. But hear this, you will, in the allowance of, see more also, feel more also this so. (**Thursday 22nd September 2022**)

And this message also mentions the 'loop pattern' that some people are finding themselves in, which I had referred to in my Telegram message. I feel there is a different pattern emerging – different, that is, from the loop pattern. And this is one of a build up of chaotic energies that are needed to push us over a tipping point threshold. This is the same process/mechanism that occurs in complex systems (and wasn't it a 'coincidence' that I did my PhD on social complex systems...??). In a complex system, as it develops, expands, and takes on greater complexity, it often reaches a stage known as a 'tipping point.' At this stage, the system can go one of two ways: it can either breakthrough or breakdown. In order to breakthrough, the system needs to gain an extra amount of energy to push it through the threshold. Yet as this extra energy emerges within the system, it creates disruption and chaos. This energetic disruption is sometimes called a 'chaotic disruptor' or 'chaos attractor' as, like a vortex, it attracts more energy to it, thus fuelling its energetic state. Eventually, this energy reaches its own tipping point where it feeds into the complex system, pushing it past the threshold into a new recombination: a newly ordered complex system of greater stability and order. If this 'push' is not reached, the chaotic energy instead activates a breakdown of the system (this is a basic overview of complex systems).

Another way to frame this is that humanity can go through the portal (threshold), or fall into the hole (breakdown). This is exactly how White Eagle of the Hopi Indigenous tells it. This is his advice:

"This moment humanity is going through can now be seen as a portal and as a hole. The decision to fall into the hole or go through the portal is up to you.

If you repent of the problem and consume the news 24 hours a day, with little energy, nervous all the time, with pessimism, you will fall into the hole. But if you take this opportunity to look at yourself, rethink life and death, take care of yourself and others, you will cross the portal. Take care of your homes, take care of your body. Connect with your spiritual House.

When you are taking care of yourselves, you are taking care of everything else. Do not lose the spiritual dimension of this crisis; have the eagle aspect from above and see the whole; see more broadly.

There is a social demand in this crisis, but there is also a spiritual demand -- the two go hand in hand. Without the social dimension, we fall into fanaticism. But without the spiritual dimension, we fall into pessimism and lack of meaning. You were prepared to go through this crisis. Take your toolbox and use all the tools available to you.

Learn about the resistance of the indigenous and African peoples; we have always been, and continue to be, exterminated. But we still haven't stopped singing, dancing, lighting a fire, and having fun. Don't feel guilty about being happy during this difficult time.

You do not help at all being sad and without energy. You help if good things emanate from the Universe now. It is through joy that one resists. Also, when the storm passes, each of you will be very important in the reconstruction of this new world.

You need to be well and strong. And for that, there is no other way than to maintain a beautiful, happy, and bright vibration. This has nothing to do with alienation.

This is a resistance strategy. In shamanism, there is a rite of passage called the quest for vision. You spend a few days alone in the forest, without water, without food, without protection. When you cross this portal, you get a new vision of the world, because you have faced your fears, your difficulties.

This is what is asked of you:

Allow yourself to take advantage of this time to perform your vision-seeking rituals. What world do you want to build for you? For now, this is what you can do -- serenity in the storm. Calm down, pray every day. Establish a routine to meet the sacred every day.

Good things emanate; what you emanate now is the most important thing. And sing, dance, resist through art, joy, faith, and love."

- White Eagle of the Hopi

Our time is approaching. Yet until we arrive at that moment of the 'psychic revolution,' we will first need to walk a rocky road. Like the camel in the desert, by keeping an eye on the horizon, it doesn't stumble for it sees ahead to what is coming rather than focusing down at its feet. This can be our vision too. We see ahead. We look further, beyond the present. We perceive into the distance to our destination rather than being distracted by the stones at our feet. And we shall get there as we step over the pebbles.

Let each of us prepare for this approaching threshold by being receptive to those energies that shall push us beyond the 'chaotic attractor' rather than being attracted to the chaos. The portal or the hole is the choice that awaits us.

The Natives are Restless:
Life in the Existential Zone

'As the interpretation of reality by the power structure,
ideology is always subordinated ultimately to the interests of
the structure. Therefore, it has a natural tendency to disengage
itself from reality, to create a world of appearances,
to become ritual.'

Vaclav Havel - *The Power of the Powerless*

There is little sense in trying to fathom what is the 'rational' in today's world. The threshold from a realm of rationality has been crossed, and we have entered the Theatre of the Absurd. Nothing seems to make sense; or rather, no one in authority is now trying to appear rational or making sense. The façade of sense-making has been dropped because everyone knows the consensus narrative is based upon a lie and even those upholding it cannot be bothered any longer to uphold the lie. It is as if the irrational has become the new standardization, so why bother to pretend things are otherwise?

The very act of living a sane life has become a revolutionary act. It is revolutionary in that mental, emotional, and psychological clarity is a rebellion against the brain fog of the consensus status quo. And yet, without such clarity of perception and insight we are in danger of becoming redundant in an environment of ever-increasing meaninglessness. An undeclared nihilism has taken root within the circuitry of the human condition and is spreading as a silent contagion. This is now the maelstrom of the times that faces so many of us – the natives are restless, and this is life in the *existential zone*.

The act of living implies that each individual gains enough meaning and purpose to keep everyday life functioning. Yet lurking behind this as a background fear in our lives is the possibility that there could be a collapse into total meaninglessness where nothing makes sense anymore. And worst of all, those around you seem not to recognize this, nor want to acknowledge it. Your sense of meaning has collapsed for you alone. This is perhaps why so many people appear to be scurrying through their lives, scrambling to clutch onto the threads of some contrived meaning or purpose. Reality, a make-believe funfair, is teetering on the edge of an abyss of abstraction. And this current uncertainty makes us all feel panicky. We never fully realized that *we* were here to decide upon our reality. We have been sitting back, consuming someone else's reality, and calling it our own. Somewhere along the way, the human species got stripped of its intentionality and its *will to purpose*.

The English writer and philosopher Colin Wilson was correct in spotting this loss of inner vitality. He related it to a rise in a need for security and by people enclosing themselves within their own walls, whether physical or mental. Wilson remarked that: 'Too much security becomes boredom, and boredom leads to a decline in vitality. Man has surrounded himself by walls, and has built his narrow "human world" as a centre of security; but the security has begun to stifle him.'[29] Whether security or insecurity, certainty and uncertainty, both sides of the coin are being used to form an enclosure around the human being. And this creates the sense of being stifled. The focus has been upon the minutiae – the details, the micro – with a loss of the macro or larger, expanded vision. We are conditioned to live for crumbs rather than feasts. This has given humanity precise technological devices that we spend our waking hours staring into, yet it has shredded the awe and exploration into the larger questions of existence. Humankind has, largely speaking, stepped into an existential zone of its own making; we have voluntarily cut ourselves off from our inherent vital energies and are living off a pocket generator. By living our lives within a thin sliver of consciousness and denying the potential of accessing a wider scope of perceptual awareness, we are existing in a kind of 'sub-threshold' state. It is as if by living we are forgetting – or that we are living in a state of forgetfulness. And this then gets perpetuated

· · · · · · · · · · · ·

29 Wilson, Colin (2019/1966) *Introduction to The New Existentialism.* London: Aristeia Press, p109

by routines and habits that establish a regular everyday overfamiliarity to life, which then leads to increased automation of oneself.

I am suggesting that life in the *existential zone* is based on the recognition that ordinary everyday human consciousness is experienced within a highly reduced and limited form. Further, that this restricted human consciousness is accepted by most people and not questioned, even though it results from certain deliberate external conditions such as social programming and cultural_institutions. We have learnt not to question the limited state of our conscious awareness. And it is this that has led humanity into a life of reduced cognition regarding our place within the grander scheme of universal awareness. For most of us, we live our lives as if within a fishbowl. Or to use another analogy, the world is like a huge 'dark room,' and we navigate our steps through crude external stimuli. As Wilson characterized it: 'The countries of the mind may be vast, but man cannot get a visa to stay there.'[30] Yet the thing is, we could get a visa *if only we applied for it ourselves*. The expansive consciousness field is in permanent existence, only that we do not make any efforts to reach out to it by shifting away from our place of restricted awareness. Why is this so? I doubt if there is any one answer for this but rather a confluence of factors. A primary factor is that we are never

. . . .

30 Wilson, Colin (2019/1966) *Introduction to The New Existentialism.* London: Aristeia Press, p123

told that anything else exists beyond the limited range of matter-reality. We have been taught by our 'knowledge institutions' that consciousness is a by-product of our brain and is only a result of our neuronal connections and it finishes with the death of the body. In other words, we have been conditioned into a belief set that there is 'nothing out there' beyond what is basically in front of our noses. And so, we tend to go through life with these adopted blinkers over our perceptive awareness. Rather than making efforts to go beyond our current state of awareness, we end up struggling for meaning through material gains. And when we achieve what we have told ourselves is our aim, we quickly become restless again. We never perceive that there is a threshold of human consciousness. We don't need to go out seeking 'mystical experiences' either, for this is likely to keep us on the merry-go-round of attractions as spiritual tourists. Like a roller coaster, we reach a peak, get a high, then it's a fast track down again before seeking the next summit. There are thrills in this, yet there is no permanence of insight. Such rides and rituals, of which our lives are full of, serve to keep our attention and awareness narrowed, and any aspects lying beyond the narrowing get excluded.

Life in the *existential zone* is all about following the noise rather than the signal and excluding all those aspects that do not fall (or are accepted) into the mainstream, consensus narrative. Exclusion then becomes a habit with us, and most people are unawares of this. If we are asked – do you feel authentic? – then how is a person to respond?

Do we have any sense of discernment to know, truly know, when we are authentic or not? And if so, then how are we inauthentic? Why is it that we ask so few questions about the fundamentals of our own existence? It would seem that there is a form of forgetfulness that hangs over us in this realm, as if we are being compelled to remain as dreamers. The act of remembrance is a theme that runs through many ancient traditions and teachings. In his theory of *anamnesis,* Plato says humanity possesses knowledge of its past, only that we have forgotten this knowledge and so we need to rediscover the knowledge within us. Plato wrote that humanity could only know the 'real world' in the form of memories. That is, human thought was really a form of recollection, and that humankind generally existed within a state of collective amnesia, having only fragments of recollection as reference points for reality. Plato was suggesting that humanity had lost – or fallen from – an earlier state of heightened awareness and now had only traces of this memory in their collective psyche as a reminder. In ancient Greek, truth is called *aletheia* which means not forgetting; and in Greek mythology, before the human soul incarnates into this world it drinks from Lethe, the river of Forgetfulness and one of the five rivers of the underworld, so that it cannot remember its origins. Similarly, there is a Jewish legend that speaks of how we are struck on the mouth by an angel before birth so that we cannot speak of our pre-birth knowledge.

Such myths and tales as these are suggesting to us that we need to learn how to *remember* – that knowledge beyond our normal ken is re-collection as much as it is cognition. We arrive in this earthly realm with an inheritance, only that we lack the key to unlock those restrictions placed upon us so that we can access expanded awareness and knowledge. We need to find the Ariadne thread within this *existential zone* to help us through this labyrinth or perceptual maze that we find ourselves in. Our lives are attempts at entering once again into a lost remembrance which lies so far and yet so close to us. The 13th century Persian poet Jalal al-Din Rumi wrote that 'The Truth is closer to us than our own jugular vein.' And yet, so vain do we search, as if we have fallen away from true remembrance. If we make no efforts, then we shall remain in ignorance to our existence. We shall play the game as pawns being moved around a chessboard, unknowing of the hands that move us. The sense of human life will be measured by the few material gains and pleasures we have obtained before the exit door approaches. We shall leave this arena having no true gains. Having failed to learn of why we came, we may end up exiting through a revolving door only to be thrown back into the game again. We have been programmed with the nice little adage that 'Ignorance is Bliss,' and then offered some of those temptations of bliss to feed upon. Yet a world that exists in ignorance shall never find its true way forward. It will stumble and fall and flail about blindly. It is time for us to *see* the condition of life; to understand how the consensus narrative is generated and manipulated; how people are kept in ignorance of their true origins and capacities; and finally, how to activate those organs that will allow us to receive a greater portion of consciousness. And with that greater conscious awareness, we can make steps to break from our restrictions and to take the helm of our lives.

The Hidden Forces of Life (Pt.1):
Influences from a Lesser Reality

For my consciousness the whole life upon earth, including the human life and all its mentality, is a mass of vibrations, mostly vibrations of falsehood, ignorance and disorder, in which are more and more at work vibrations of Truth and Harmony coming from the higher regions and pushing their way through the resistance.

The Mother

Sleep is very comfortable, but waking is very bitter.

G.I. Gurdjieff

It is a natural, yet incorrect, assumption to accept physical events at face value. Influences come to us upon many varied levels, and the visible, physical carrier or medium is the most superficial form. All of life is a play of forces; we may call these 'universal forces' for they act both within and beyond the physical. We have become accustomed to giving personal forms to many of these forces, and we believe that we are independent and free from their influence. The Greek-Armenian mystic G.I. Gurdjieff used to say that humankind lives under 48 laws, of which they are mostly unaware or ignorant of. This is a very precise number, and it is not the numbers – the quantity – or the specifics that I wish to focus on here, but the *quality*. It may be necessary to have a 'feeling' for the forces of influence that populate our lives in the physical domain.

Most people, most of the time, are not aware of the forces acting upon them; and this is a natural condition. We all live our lives within a sea of vibrations – thoughts, suggestions, influences, etc – and we are barely aware of which ones belong to us and which we take to be our own. Let us take a common example as an illustration: information. When a person receives information, the general response is to consider the likelihood of that information in relation to their belief sets and range of accumulated opinions. The person then makes a response regarding whether the information is 'true' or 'false.' Yet this is a limited two-dimensional way to regard the relationship of the communication. We have to also consider the background to the source of the information: what is the source; do they have an agenda; are they relaying the information from another source; what is the motivation; what are the expected outcomes? And more. We may also need to ask ourselves whether the medium of transmission is reliable or corrupted. If a technological medium is used, are there subtle subliminal messages and signalling within the transmission? Are certain frequencies being used to manipulate the hearer? Is the receiver being discreetly nudged into making desired outcomes? If this is a face-to-face communication, we may also ask whether the speaker is using specific techniques of language coercion, such as neuro-linguistic programming? These are just a very few of the potential influences that could be used in the physical communication of information. And yet, these are still those forces of influence that are limited to the physical range. It is good to be mindful that non-physical forces compete for power the same as familiar physical forces do. What is hidden to us in everyday life are the motivations behind the impulses that surface within the physical.

The human life experience conditions us to view and respond to outward aspects whilst remaining unaware of those things acting behind the veil – or behind the scenes. This disjuncture between *origin* and *target* is more than a gap; it is a gulf. As the Indian philosopher Sri Aurobindo remarked in relation to the hidden forces of life, 'the only way out is through the descent of a consciousness which is not the puppet of these forces but is greater than they are and can compel them either to change or disappear.'[31] Aurobindo is saying here that the 'way out' is not to attempt to fight or meet these forces head on but to align with a degree of consciousness that is greater, or vibrationally beyond, the level of those forces. Rather than struggle with them, we are to resonate to a different vibrational alignment that takes us out of their spectrum of influence.

• • • • • • • • • • • • •

31 *Hidden Forces of Life: Selections from the Works of Sri Aurobindo and the Mother* (Lotus Press, 1999), p6

Within the general scheme of things, most people are treated as ignorant instruments; they are moved around like puppets, suspecting nothing. They live predictable lives; that is, lives that can be predicted as they move within known patterns. Often, these patterns are what have been programmed into the collective mass society. As soon as a person shifts to an inner-directed life, they begin to move away from predictability. That is, they move 'off-pattern,' and this is not well-liked by those of the governing forces. The spirit-consciousness can override the lower forces, which is why the earthly life is being increasingly pulled into a physical-material direction – a pathway to both outer as well as inner automation. Stability is based on a repetition of vibrations and frequencies that our being becomes accustomed to. A person gets entrained through vibrational alignment into a mode of stability. The question we should be asking ourselves is: what type of frequencies are we aligning with? A great deal of stability within the physical realm is of a 'lower order' type, based on more limited patterns. Some may wonder, what is all this talk about vibrations – isn't that new age nonsense? It all depends on how such information is presented and conveyed. A truth can easily be made into a mockery if handled incorrectly. The Serbian inventor Nikola Tesla famously said: 'If you want to find the secrets of the universe, think in terms of energy, frequency and vibration.' Again, going back to G.I. Gurdjieff, who stated:

It is necessary to regard the universe as consisting of vibrations. These vibrations proceed in all kinds, aspects, and densities of the matter which constitutes the universe, from the finest to the coarsest...In this instance the view of ancient knowledge is opposed to that of contemporary science, because at the base of the understanding of vibrations ancient knowledge places the principle of the discontinuity of vibrations. The principle of the discontinuity of vibrations means the definite and necessary characteristic of all vibrations in nature, whether ascending or descending, to develop not uniformly but with periodical accelerations and retardations.[32]

It is interesting here that Gurdjieff speaks about the 'discontinuity of vibrations' that develop through periodical accelerations (increases) and retardations (delays). There is not a uniformity in the influence of vibrations. The 'energetic background' of life, so to speak, moves through these periodic shifts. This can be seen as a macro influence upon human life. In such times, we may feel irritable, restless, frustrated, or more. Philosopher J.G. Bennett referred to this when he wrote:

• • • • • • • • • • • • •

32 P. D. Ouspensky, *In Search of the Miraculous: Fragments of an Unknown Teaching* (New York: Harcourt Brace and World, 1949), 122-23

In a more subtle and pervasive manner, great regions of the earth's surface, and sometimes even the whole of the earth, become subject to a state of tension that produces in people a strong sense of dissatisfaction with their conditions of life. They become irritable or aggressive, apprehensive, nervous and highly suggestible.[33]

These impersonal forces that influence the world, and our states of being, we know only by the results they cause. We perceive only a small degree through the lens of visible events and consequences. There are forces unknown to us that are responsible for shaping our physical, psychic, and emotional environment. The human being lives 'constantly in the midst of a whirl of unseen mind-forces and life-forces of which we know nothing, we are not even aware of their existence.'[34]

There are currently forces acting upon human consciousness and producing a great deal of pressure. We are in need of an outlet for this pressure, before it implodes/explodes through our societies in uncomfortable and disagreeable ways. There is now a contestation of forces that are so visible that they can no longer be denied by

• • • • • • • • • • • •

33 Bennett, J.G. 1989. *Is There "Life" on Earth? - An Introduction to Gurdjieff.* Santa Fe, NM: Bennett Books, p31

34 *Hidden Forces of Life: Selections from the Works of Sri Aurobindo and the Mother* (Lotus Press, 1999), p81

the aware (or awake) individual. At the same time, a great evolutionary (developmental) force is pushing into the earthly domain, and there is immense resistance to this. This makes the struggle – the contestation of forces – more acute, more violent, and more definitive. Yet this very visibility of the counterforces upon the physical world stage is an important sign for us – it displays their state of desperation to come out of the shadows in this way. This opens up an important path of realization for the rest of us – and possibilities too. Even if individual transformation is upon a small scale, there is the opportunity now for a general uplifting within collective humanity. And it is this general uplifting that will usher in the potentials and conditions for a new world to emerge. Again, as Bennett says,

> If a new world is to come, we must first create it in ourselves. You may ask how the work of a few people can change the world. It has always been so. Ideas are powerful, not organizations. Nothing can be done by outward force; everything can be done by inner strength.[35]

We have arrived at an exceptional hour, a privileged time for the expansion of human awareness and perception, *if only we can bypass those forces of hindrance*. What we need

• • • • • • • • • • • •

35 Bennett, J.G. 1989. *Is There "Life" on Earth? - An Introduction to Gurdjieff.* Santa Fe, NM: Bennett Books, p32

now is inner certitude and to exercise discernment – especially when open to the forces of mass vibration.

The Forces of Mass Vibration

The mass exhibits a different resonance than the individual. When in a group, or crowd, an individual invariably takes on the features, thoughts, and moods of others. In this way, the individual can be inwardly polluted and corrupted by forces they are not aware of. It is important to be conscious of who we choose to be with, mix with, for each person is a point of reception/ transmission, and we vibrationally align (resonate) with those we are physically close to. That is why the mob can be psychologically, and behaviourally, dangerous. And this is also why we are advised to choose our friends carefully; a lot can be said about a person according to their friends and associates. It would do us well to remember that 'one catches the constant contagion of all desires, all the lower movements, all the small obscure reactions, all the unwanted vibrations which come to us from those around us.'[36] Life is a continual interplay of forces, a continuous alchemy in which a person is constantly absorbing various kinds of vibration that may contain all types of possible dissonance. In this, the task of the conscious and aware person is to transmute these dissonant forces so

36 *Hidden Forces of Life: Selections from the Works of Sri Aurobindo and the Mother* (Lotus Press, 1999), p185

that their action and influence is disabled. We can do this by *grounding* the vibration. Let us say that something, an event, a person, or a comment, has caused us frustration. We refrain from responding to it by taking an inner pause, an internal step back, and we observe the discomfort. This 'item' is treated as an observable object with a life of its own – it is an energy form. And it needs to be allowed to dissipate rather than find an energy source to latch onto (i.e., oneself). In this, the energy form (the 'item') needs to be grounded within neutral physicality – just as electricity or lightening needs to be grounded or 'earthed.' Similarly, we *earth* the dissonant energy by visualizing its transference into the ground beneath us (it doesn't matter if you are sitting or standing). In this way, the dissonant energy vibration is transmuted. This action is the work of perceptive consciousness and does not have to be regarded as something 'spiritual.' On the contrary, it is part of the task of the human being during its sojourn through physical life to transmute energies. It is through the presence of conscious individuals that, according to the Mother (Sri Aurobindo's spiritual co-worker), a 'minimum of general harmony' can be accomplished:

> That presence, that spiritual light – which could almost be called a spiritual consciousness – is within each being and all things, and because of it, in spite of all discordance, all passion, all violence, there is a minimum of general harmony which

allows Nature's work to be accomplished.[37]

It is through such Work as this that we become aware of the intervention of forces, impulses, and influences, which are non-visible to our ordinary states of consciousness, and which seek to affect physical life circumstances.

The forces of mass vibrational dissonance are exceptionally intense in these current times. It can be said that humanity has reached a particular state of general tension. Such 'forces of hindrance' would delight in creating divisions by dividing friendships and social alliances. Some divisions, however, are set to occur, for these are the breakdowns in the dysfunctional external systems that perpetuate the fractures in our societies. These are such systems as politics, economy, and social trust. We can expect some cracks to appear in these systems for 'Nature's Work' to operate. Yet we cannot allow these fractures to disable the human spirit – or to numb the forces of spirit-consciousness that act through us. As stated by the Mother in the opening citation to this essay, life is mostly awash with vibrations of disorder and falsehood, in which 'vibrations of Truth and Harmony are coming from the higher regions and pushing their way through the resistance.' We are tasked, in these times, to assist these 'vibrations of Truth and Harmony' and to help them to push their way through the resistance. And in this,

· · · · · · · · · · · ·

37 *Hidden Forces of Life: Selections from the Works of Sri Aurobindo and the Mother* (Lotus Press, 1999), p167

we are aligning with the continuation of the alchemical work by assisting in the transmutation of the dissonance (the lead) into constructive forces (the gold). And by doing this we shall also be assisting in the alchemical transmutation of the great treasure of the philosopher's stone – *ourselves*.

The Hidden Forces of Life (Pt.2):
Techne & Terraforming

'We must learn to recognize what is working in the world and respond accordingly for the sake of the world.'

Rudolf Steiner

As human civilization passes further into a materialized existence, particular forces shall arise that find their domain within such an environment. That is, each epoch of civilization contends with forces, known and unknown, according to humanity's state of development, awareness, and in correspondence to the form of existing cultures and societal structures. Forces that impinge and participate within human life in this realm do so relative to the time and place. In other words, it can be said that consistent forces involved within the evolutionary journey of humanity are consistently adapting according to the epoch. Human life upon this planet is now transitioning into an era of techne (techne). In its original sense, in Greek philosophy, this term signified the mechanical arts; whilst Aristotle viewed techne as representing the imperfection of the human imitation of nature. That is, the mechanical arts were imperfect in attempting to imitate, reproduce, and/or substitute the processes of Nature. The mechanical arts also represented not only the mechanical objects/structures themselves but also the sets of ordered practices and skills that went along with them. In other words, techne is not only, in modern terms, a piece of technology, but also the behaviour, lifestyle practices, attitudes, skill sets, and more, than run alongside, or are instigated, by technology in order for its inclusion into human life. If human behaviour becomes more automated by a piece of technology, such as the use of a spell-checker (as is being used here), then the laziness in personal grammar that results from this is also a part of the techne of the computer and word processing software. What I am saying here is that the direction that humanity is taking, in the name of progress, is towards establishing a new environmental infrastructure that will reorganize and recalibrate human behaviour. It will also require a readaptation as this is not a minor transition, such as a generational linear progression, but a major transformation in how life is experienced upon this planet. Human adaptation also requires an adaptation in consciousness.

Each aeon, or major period of history, brings with it a particular mode of consciousness. For example, the Swiss philosopher Jean Gebser noted how human consciousness is not continuous but is in transition; and that these transitions, or switching of modes, are not continuous but rather 'mutations.' They undergo a leap, or jump – a sometimes radical switching – that is not linear. Gebser outlined the following consciousness structures: i) the archaic; ii) the magical; iii) the mythical; iv) the mental; and v) the integral. Each of these structures framed how people perceived the world around them and the forces within it. Such consciousness structures also influenced how particular worldviews, behaviours, and environments emerged. At each stage, *how* we think affects what we create. Since humanity has now, according to Gebser, entered into the 'integral structure,' then this is being projected into how our cultures and civilizations are being reconstructed. The world-building of each aeon of history is influenced by the incumbent structure of human consciousness (which is itself influenced by cosmic factors).[38] According to Gebser, the integral consciousness structure was made evident by a new relationship to space and time. In some ways, we can see how this is manifesting through our increasingly digitalized cultures that have drastically altered how people experience space-time relations. Consciousness, and intelligence, are themselves unseen (and often unrecognized) forces that have huge influence upon human life. Conversely, how an environment is built-up also then reflects back certain influences and impacts upon a person's consciousness. A very basic analogy here is the difference between being immersed in Nature, in a natural environment,

• • • • • • • • • • • •

38 See Richard Tarnas's monumental work *Cosmos and Psyche: Intimations of a New World View* (2006)

as opposed to being immersed within a high-density urban environment. In this context, the human being is now being exposed not only to a digitized ecosystem but also to an unprecedented electromagnetic one. We are literally existing within a sea of unseen, and hidden, forces. It can be said that the planet is undergoing a mode of *terraforming*. And the 'form' that is under construction will be amenable to a certain type of intelligence. For starters, it will be kind to an intelligence that understands how to use digital tools, apps, and software. And it will be unkind to those intelligences that find it difficult to get their heads around all this 'online stuff.' It will be kind to those who are willing to accept a life 'within the grid' of digital-everything – finances, surveillance, internet-of-bodies, 5G/6G/7G/8G, etc – and it will be unkind to those wishing for an off-grid, or less digitally-dense, lifestyle.

For some, what is being described here is the shift into transhumanism, alongside the rise of a civilizational technocracy. What is also being described is a new mode of materialism that does not need to rely on physical solidity for it to be material, as the immersion into the physical-digital ecosystem is still a mode of materialism, albeit more ethereal. I have referred to this as the 'material fallacy' that represents a reterritorializing of physical matter. This fallacy is that the continuing encapsulation of the human being into artificial constructs (such as the Metaverse) is a deepening deception of materiality. And such an environment also affects the cognitive functioning of the mind as it becomes ever more deeply immersed into an electrified realm. This will designate the new domain of techne where different cognitive skills will be necessary. It will also frame how humanity is tracked, monitored, catalogued, and processed. Humanity will become symbiotic. New processes of integration are being established between the biological world, the digital, and the electronic. What may be emerging here is a wholly different form of planetization that merges genes, machines, and societies. The human intelligence that will result from this is, as yet, unformed and, in most ways, unknown. And it may become home to more than one form of intelligence. As I have mentioned previously, there is the danger that as people slip further into an ecosystem of automation, not only their behaviour but also their state of cognition will be affected. The unconscious human may, by degrees, be transformed into the *robosapien* where behaviour sets and cognitive perception are limited to a very low level. Such a person will, effectively, be little more than a cog in the machine. And the machine will be well-oiled by AI-regulated infrastructures. Yet the real 'hidden force' in such an electrified world may be something more nefarious than the automated human being.

The ongoing terraforming of the natural, organic world opens itself up for a replacement by a 'machinic civilization' based on technocratic governance and processes of techne. When the ecosystems of Nature are broken down, reduced to material systems, then the building blocks for artificial structures – structures devoid of organic life – are established which give host for the manifestation

153

and expression of anti-developmental forces (or what I sometimes refer to as *entropic forces*). The present times are hyper-materialistic and heavily intellect dominant. This allows for an organization of human thinking where free speech, human imagination and intuition, is highly controlled and subjected to monitoring, management, and technocratic administration. If this continues then it is likely to lead to a state where the human species, unknowing to itself, will have lost the ability for true, genuine thinking. The inner world will have become diminished, and any inner, developmental impulses become over-ridden by material forces. Furthermore, we may be oblivious to the many unseen fields that make up our ecosystem of electro-energies. These energies are sub-nature. They are part of living existence, yet they are a lower form of life vibration. According to Austrian mystic-philosopher Rudolf Steiner, electricity is light in a *sub-material* state. That is, it is a form of light that has fallen below the level of nature and has become what he termed 'sub-nature.' It is because of this that Steiner warned humankind to be cautious not to build cultures dependent or based on electricity. An electro-ecosystem will only serve to draw us farther away from our natural environments and into a lower vibrational state of sub-nature. In a lecture from 1925, Steiner says

> There are very few as yet who even feel the greatness of the spiritual tasks approaching man in this direction. Electricity, for instance,

celebrated since its discovery as the very soul of Nature's existence, must be recognised in its true character — in its peculiar power of leading down from Nature to Sub Nature. Only man himself must beware lest he slide downward with it.[1]

Rudolf Steiner made great efforts to outline aspects of the various forces acting against humankind's development. One of these forces he termed as *ahrimanic*, and the intention of these forces was to draw humanity into their realm; that is, to drag human beings further into deep material entanglement.

It can be said that those forces that wish for deeper immersion into materialism (whether physical or digital) are entropic forces for they act against the inner development of the human being. And for the large part, they are unseen or hidden. For Steiner, Ahriman is a very real intelligent being, or form of intelligence, and it represents a realm (or reality) that is dry, mechanistic, intellectual, devoid of vital energies (what we would call as 'spirit' or 'soul') and may even be devoid of organic life. What this intelligence – these *ahrimanic forces* – strive for is to persuade humankind that such a mechanistic environment is good for them. Not only this, but also that such a thing is positive, necessary, and even progressive. The goal here is to present such events as the best direction for the future of human evolution. In a nutshell, think transhumanism. The advent for such forces to ingratiate themselves into an electrified realm of sub-nature is being prepared by an Earthly environment where electricity is replacing our need for genuine light, and chemical skies are increasingly blocking the reception of the sunlight. Furthermore, such forces, being highly materialistic, are primarily focused upon the dominance of an economic realm; a reality where humans are coerced into thinking of economy as the main driver and principal concern. The focus is upon the quantity and not the quality, exemplified by a culture that is governed by numbers, statistics, algorithms, data harvesting, and evidence-based proof. It is these unseen forces of cataloguing, identifying, and accrediting (see also the China-led social credit score system) that are dividing people away from their natural, organic relations.

Many cultures are already separated by 'identity divisions' – social, racial, and sexual – that are encouraging strife and polarizations within our societies. Whatever separates groups, keeps people from mutual understanding and divides them, can be utilized to support the entropic forces. It is precisely within human divisions where antagonistic forces are more likely to intervene. As Steiner wrote in his notebook in November 1920: '*Where are the ahrimanic forces? They are there where forces separating people can intervene*'.[2] As I have said, we do not need to personify such forces here, only to recognize the presence of counter developmental forces that, through whatever function, are hostile to the inner growth and perceptive capacities of the human being. In this respect, the greatest danger is that people are sleeping through these times; as such, they remain ignorant or unaware of such forces operating within their midst. To be conscious of such forces, and the instruments/vessels through which such forces operate, is paramount now so that we are not seduced by these impulses unknowingly, and thus do not unwittingly become their puppets. Also, it is through awareness and knowing that such forces can be transformed into serving humanity by compelling individuals into increased understanding and a wish for development and a betterment of the human condition. It is through increasing awareness that people are able to see how seemingly 'good intentions' are being hijacked by groups (political, financial, social, etc.) to become tools and channels for nefarious intentions and goals.

The terraforming of modern life, through techne (automatism) and technocratic governance, is having the result of desensitizing people and separating them from the realm of vital, creative forces. People's thoughts have become more and more like dead shadows – opinions that mimic social programming, limited attention spans, and cognitive dissonance. For some time now, human intelligence has been instrumentalized, splintered, and fractured so as to produce an increased sense of alienation from the natural world and from connection with the inner being's *elan vital* (vital spirit). Yet, it may be that we have to encounter such forces in these times in order to make choices regarding our own path of development. It is this present encounter, however, that is causing dissonance amongst so many people in the world today. If a person falls too much into materialism, distraction, psycho-emotional fog, then this can result in a number of factors such as automatism, instability, depression, anxiety, and a general state of disquietude. In short, they become detached from the inner being.

Furthermore, the deepening entanglement with a technological ecosystem is driving people into sub-nature and lower states of consciousness. In such cultural circumstances as we find ourselves in, people need to dig deeper to find the inner strength in order not to be overwhelmed by these external forces. It is precisely through conscious discernment that we can find the inner strength to face the conditions of the world. It is this discernment that will enable an individual to see through the manufactured narratives that are programming people into supporting the external forces of 'efficiency,' 'rationality,' and 'progressiveness,' that are seemingly more and more anti-human. As one recent popular cultural historian said: 'People will no longer regard themselves as autonomous beings who follow their own wishes according to their life, but rather as a collection of biochemical mechanisms that are constantly monitored and directed by a network of electronic algorithms.'[3] Such ideas, agendas, and their supporting forces, view the human being as a component within a technical system; that is, as part of the processes of techne. And through this perspective, the human being is a flawed creature that requires to be technologically improved. Again, this is a view that moves further and further away from the understanding of the human being as a vessel of spirit – as a manifestation of Source-consciousness within a physical body. These are part of the unseen forces of life that are acting through, and orchestrating, physical events across the planet. One Anthroposophical[39] researcher and writer even went as far as to state the following:

> Ahriman's objective of the comprehensive capture in digital form of all human souls and bodies on Earth, their "digital identity", requires the biometric capture of every individual, their immunization and other data, right into their molecular structure, and was planned and already set in motion some time ago with the aim of creating a universal health information system.'[4]

A destiny such as this lies upon a path of ignorance and an abandonment of the inner life. Such a future can only come about by the continual accumulation of present trends acting one upon the other to form a stairway to a determined end. If this is seen as destiny, then it is one that emerges through either ignorance or laziness. In other words, it is through purely physical circumstances and does not accept or acknowledge the presence of metaphysical truths. It is within such a barren landscape,

• • • • • • • • • • • •

39 Anthroposophy is a spiritual-science movement founded in the early 20th century by the mystic-philosopher Rudolf Steiner.

devoid of the transcendental impulse, that such entropic forces can pry and play upon the weaknesses of an unseeing, unperceiving humanity. There are unseen, hidden forces in life that are striving for such anti-human ambitions – yet it is their lack of grace and vital energy that also is their greatest weakness.

For individuals – especially those with perceptive capacity and compassionate understanding – to walk into the future blind to such forces and their influences shall be our greatest weakness. That is why there are tremendous efforts to keep as many people as possible unawares to events beyond the programmed narrative. As the opening quote from Rudolf Steiner says, we must learn to recognize what is working in the world so that we have the capacity to respond accordingly for the sake of the world. For this is our human world, and there is no place in it for anti-human forces.

References

[1] Rudolf Steiner, "From Nature to Sub-Nature," *Anthroposophical Leading Thoughts* - https://wn.rsarchive.org/Books/GA026/English/RSP1973/GA026_c29.html

[2] Selg, Peter (2022) *The Future of Ahriman and the Awakening of Souls*. Forest Row: Temple Lodge Publishing, p53

[3] Yuval Noah Harari, cited in Selg, Peter (2022) *The Future of Ahriman and the Awakening of Souls*. Forest Row: Temple Lodge

Publishing, p49

[4] Selg, Peter (2022) *The Future of Ahriman and the Awakening of Souls*. Forest Row: Temple Lodge Publishing, p44

The Hidden Forces of Life (Pt.3):
The Understanding of Light & Darkness

'The profound thought that lies in this is that the kingdom of darkness has to be overcome by the kingdom of light, not by means of punishment, but through mildness; not by resisting evil, but by uniting with it in order to redeem evil as such. Because a part of the light enters into evil, the evil itself is overcome.'

Rudolf Steiner (November 11th, 1904)

It was noted in the previous essay ('The Hidden Forces of Life, Pt.2') how each aeon, or major period of history, brings with it a particular mode of consciousness; and each of these periods framed how people perceived the world around them and the forces within it. Such periods establish what we may call 'consciousness structures' (reality or belief sets) that then influence the worldviews, behaviours, and environments that emerge from this. This affects how cultures and communities are formed; how value systems are agreed upon; and other moral and ethical implications. In each period there are varying frameworks for how concepts such as 'good' and 'bad,' for example, are viewed. What was once accepted as a 'good thing' or an 'evil thing' change over time and in relation to our social-cultural groupings. At each period of human history, the contestations between the 'good' and the 'bad' take place within the emblems and motifs of the time. This is one of the constant struggles within the emergence of material existence. Similarly, certain human values are conditioned and promoted within cultures as part of their exterior growth, such as killing in the name of your culture/king/ leader, etc. Even today, such values are much misaligned for there are people who still hold conditioning belief sets that value religious martyrdom or killing in the name of one's country (warfare) as a positive good. Phenomena remains largely consistent, yet the mode of interpretation shifts according to the time, the place, and the people.

This relationship of phenomena and its shifting interpretation can also be seen in regard to energies and forces – in other words, as non-personified forms. Since remotest antiquity the polarity or dualistic struggle within existence has been framed as the Light vs. the Dark. This is a verifiable distinction as all materiality exhibits these light/dark distinctions; from day/night; black/white; awake/asleep; alive/dead; positive/negative; active/passive, and so on. Yet these light/dark distinctions only take on their 'good' or 'bad' characteristics when designated by human beings. The atom with its positive proton and negative electron are not deemed as the 'good' proton and the 'bad' electron; rather, they are energetic dualities necessary for holding form. In other words, the classic light/dark distinctions are not to be automatically (and sloppily) categorized as being also the good/bad (or good/evil). There are, without doubt, people and actions that can be designated as evil; yet these are separate formations from the ongoing light/dark dualities. Within our manifested reality, the Light and the Dark are both necessary for life to function and to continue to evolve. In terms of Light/Dark, both principles stand opposite to each other in a way that does not allow their differences to be diminished or resolved. They are meant to exist in stark dualism. They are extreme in that their essence is contrary in equal measure to the other. Light is as light just as the dark is dark. They are essential dualisms in equal measure – a polarity of two creative principles. They are not in opposition in a hierarchical structure (i.e., one is 'higher' than the other) but as counter poles to each other. This is a dynamic dualism. It is the interaction between them that changes rather than the essence of each.

Gnostic teachings historically place the dark and light within a vertical hierarchy where the light occupies a higher state/principle as opposed to the dark. If we consider the Light/Dark as operative principles within an integrated whole – just as day and night – then neither one is essentially good nor bad/evil. Perhaps we can view how people align themselves with certain principles pertaining more to one component over the other as being a choice to join with 'good' or 'evil' aspects. We may refer to this within the framework of the spirit-matter dialectic.

The Spiritual Dialectic

In an earlier essay of mine – *Toward Synthesis* (2014)[40] – I stated how movement and change is often symbolized through struggle and opposition. In social-historical terms, there have been struggle and opposition between class relations, politics, and more, that have been the cause of varied revolutions (the revolution bringing about the 'resolution'). This notion of oppositional struggle to create a third force of resolution is known as a dialectic. That is, the thesis (force) and its antithesis (opposing force) create a synthesis (resolution). The dialectic struggle was developed by the German philosopher Georg Hegel who wrote that the mind or spirit manifested itself in a set of contradictions and oppositions that were ultimately integrated and united in synthesis. For Hegel, the synthesis (the absolute), must always pass through a stage of opposition in its journey to completion and truth. On a material level, Hegel viewed this dialectic relationship as the process by which human history unfolds. That is, history (social evolution) progresses as a struggle between two opposing forces toward a developmental state of resolution. According to Hegel, the main characteristic of resolution-in-unity was that it evolved through contradiction and denial. These struggles, says Hegel, can be found in most social domains

• • • • • • • • • • • •

40 See - https://kingsleydennis.com/toward-synthesis/

165

such as history, philosophy, art, nature, and even consciousness. Hegel's thinking was highly influenced by the lesser-known writings of German Christian mystic Jacob Böhme. Böhme's inner visions led him to create a cosmology where it was necessary for humanity to return to God. These states of conflict would be a necessary stage in the further completion of the evolution of the universe. Humanity's free will in this separation, conflict, and resolution was the most important gift that God could give to us. In other words, it would be our own responsibility – and a privileged responsibility at that – to work toward our reconciliation through struggle and the opposing forces of resistance.

In a similar manner, the teachings of Greek-Armenian philosopher-mystic George Gurdjieff also describe a dialectic relationship through the oppositional forces of *Holy Affirming* and *Holy Denying* leading to a *Holy Reconciling*. Gurdjieff referred to this as the 'Law of Three.' In this context, we can see how a coming together of contradictory impulses – such as mind and spirit – would lead to a resolution that would not only be an integration of these contradictory forces but at the same time a resolution/synthesis *greater than* the sum of its parts. This dialectical approach suggests that every idea (thesis) gives rise to a counter idea (antithesis) and the original idea and counter idea merge to give rise to a new idea (synthesis). Or, using Gurdjieff's terminology, the Holy-Affirming force attracts a Holy-Denying force, and this contestation leads to a resolution of the Holy-

Reconciling – the active, passive, and unifying (also called the neutral). Some astute commentators have recognized dialectical forces operative upon the world stage:

> The practicing "dialecticians" of secret societies and Orders know very well that if one wants to launch into a world-wide adventure on one side, it is necessary to create for oneself a counter-effect from the other side. Reduced to its simplest terms, this means that as soon as we let the dogs off the leash on one side, the same has to happen on the other; it will not work otherwise. But the one and the other have to be controlled from a unified centre.[1]

In this instance, the dialectic oppositions are overseen by an existing 'unified centre.' In some form, a 'third force' is required in order to represent a resolution. This third force could also emerge from within a mingling of the opposing forces, just as two metals coming together can form an alloy. Such an approach was described in the Manichean teachings.

The teaching of the prophet Mani – known as *Manichaeism* – proposes the two principles of light and dark as essential dualisms. According to Mani's teachings, these two dualistic principles work through three epochs.

These are: i) Non-interference between light and dark; ii) Interference between both principles and the mingling of light and darkness; iii) Separation between light and darkness.[41] A distinctive feature of Manichaeism's dualism is in its dynamic aspect – the *mingling*. These two principles are not at rest (this was only when in the first epoch of non-interference); now they are in ever-stronger interaction with one another. This intermingling is what results in matter, which incorporates both aspects of the light and dark. Mani describes this as the darkness devouring the light beings in a kind of metabolic process whereby one substance takes and integrates the other into itself. In this understanding, these dual principles are equal in their status yet opposed to each other in their nature. This means that they occupy equal rank within the participation of the creation process, and matter reality (materiality) is an infusion of the two. Without their participation, interaction, and interplay, no creation would have been possible. The collaboration of light and dark is what constitutes creation and not one without the other. What this ultimately leads to is the message that both light and darkness are necessary for the creative process. This material world is not the realm of dark forces alone, as certain Gnostic teachings posit, but is formed when light beings/energies become mingled with the darkness. Material existence is an interplay, or collaboration, between the forces/energies of light and darkness, albeit in accordance with their separate natures.

• • • • • • • • • • • •

41 This cosmology is described in the *Cologne Mani Codex*.

Yet their interaction, which can also be seen as conflict at times, is necessary for the continued evolution within matter-reality.

Why the Energies of Conflict are a Necessary Part of Growth

The light and the darkness are both aspects of creative energies in their own right. It is helpful to consider that when we engage with the exterior physical world, we are being met with contrasts and polarities. It is these contrasts that create the tangible frictions in life which enable events to unfold and develop. As it is said: nothing grows in a vacuum. Contrasts, dualisms, and polarities do not imply that they never meet (as in 'never the twain shall meet'). Instead, we can consider that these contrasts are intermingled together to form the mixture – the material reality – which is a combination of light and dark energies rather than these being stand alone, or stand offish, elements. In this, the dynamic of opposition is transformed into a dynamic of interaction. When this interaction is stabilized, we can say that the dualism is momentarily neutralized so that a balanced unity is formed where light and dark are in equilibrium. This state is only maintained for a period until a new imbalance emerges that plunges matter-reality into a new excited state of mutual dynamic interaction and the whole cycle repeats itself until a new order of equilibrium and balance is restored. At each cycle of dynamic interaction and balance, evolvement results and there is a period of development. It is from a state of heightened perception that this arrangement of duality is perceived and understood as being intrinsic to the whole unity. From a state of lower consciousness, it all appears as continual dualistic polarization. It is the intermingling of light and dark energies that allow for a transfiguration into a new condition or state. In Manichaeism, there is no 'punishment' or resistance of evil but rather a uniting with it so as to redeem evil. Because a part of the light enters into evil, the evil itself is overcome.

The Austrian mystic and philosopher Rudolf Steiner shared the Manichaean perspective in that evil forces have a role to play in creative life and evolution. What we regard as evil is not foreign or external to processes of life evolution. On the contrary, they are required and are integral to the cosmos. Such forces will also, according to both Steiner and Mani, eventually be absorbed and transfigured by the forces of light. In this sense, both forces of light and dark are eternal properties. Interestingly, Steiner also refers to evil as an 'ill-timed good' – 'What is evil? Nothing but an ill-timed good... So we see that evil is nothing else than a mis-placed good.'[42] What this also implies is that if good works (the light) begin to stagnate or turn away (delay) in its path of evolvement, it too can at the wrong moment – the 'ill-

• • • • • • • • • • • •

42 From a speech Steiner gave on November 11th, 1904 (CW 93)

timing' – turn into darkness. In a sense, life and form – spirit and matter – are aspects of the light and dark collaboration. The Manichaean intention, as it is referred to, appears to indicate a triumph of transfiguration of spirit (light) over matter (darkness). The role of the spirit-endowed human being is thus to transform the darkness through the spiritualization of matter. The inner being of the individual is here guided to overcome (and thus transform) the trappings of materialism and materiality. The continued advancement into a technologized future represents a deepening into materialism and the forces of darkness. The true light is now being opposed by the artificial light (the mimicry) of electricity (sub-Nature). As we know, technological infrastructures are fuelled/fed by electricity – the antithesis of natural light. The challenge facing humanity here is utilizing the physical body as a vessel for light (the 'light body'), potentially through a heightened energization of the bodily cells, which incidentally already emit bio-photon fields, in order to oppose the development of a 'cyborg' body enmeshed within material technology.

It may be that the drive into technology will be led by the false 'I' or persona/ego of the human being. Therefore, the transformation of the dark to light also applies to the shedding of the human ego and false personality towards the full flowering of the inner being. The inner being (the body of light) requires freedom, authenticity, and expression. The antithesis to this is the automaton – the *robosapien*. The auto-addict, disempowered, unthinking individual, is the 'slave to other' and hence a slave to unbeing. This is what the darker forces are aiming for in their radical attempt to not only desensitize and dumb down humanity but also in their intention to attach existing humans into a tech-transhumanist merger. Yet in order for the light to be activated to full potential, it is likely that the dark forces will first push their agenda to the extreme. On this, Steiner has said: 'It is necessary in the great plan that evil, too, should come to a peak ... The good would not be so great a good if it were not to grow through the conquest of evil.'[2] The recognition of this situation is what can assist in the transformative process, understanding that a spirit energy is to transfigure the heavier elements of material form. This process of transfiguration is undertaken by assimilating the forces of darkness – evil tendencies – into the human being. It has been said that: 'Humankind beings must assimilate these forces of evil, which are operative in the universe. By doing so, we implant in our being the seed to experience consciously the life of the spirit...'[3] Furthermore, the Manichaean view is that the forces of evil are gaining a continually stronger presence within the inner life of human beings. Yet this also can be regarded as a form of 'initiation' for the human individual can come to know the presence and/or power of evil within themselves as part of the process of transmutation and redemption. The beginning steps of transmutation begin through our small daily acts, and in our continual rejection of tempting thoughts and the urges toward committing even the smallest of evil deeds. Through resisting these temptations – these 'voices' in our heads – the human being is alchemizing and transmuting the presence and power of the darker forces within material life. That is why it was said that: 'The aim of Manichaeism is to sublimate human beings to become redeemers.'[43]

The spiritual dialectic, the understanding of the transmutation of darker energies, is not a theoretical or intellectual concept but only comes alive, along with the knowledge of it, through lived experience. It is out of the lived experience that new forms emerge. Life is an ever continuing and developing process. If it becomes static or stagnant, it withers into a final state of dissolution (or a non-evolutionary path). There are as many states of Ignorance as there are Knowledge – perhaps more so. It may be more accurate to say that our present physical reality is further in the grip of the darker forces than the light. Earthly systems are more geared to serving the structures of Ignorance and Falsehood. For this reason, all genuine endeavours to provide knowledge and guidance on inner development and increased perception are assaulted by the Powers of the world. And yet it is these very assaults that provide the opportunity, and impetus, for real, genuine, developmental work to take place within the human realm. As one commentator stated:

· · · · · · · · · · · ·

43 From a speech Steiner gave on May 16th, 1906 (CW 94)

This period is the greatest opportunity that has existed for many thousands of years for "the Work." Not for thousands of years has there been such a need for people who are able "to work." The reason for this is that the transition from one system to another can come only through the "third force." It cannot come from the passive majority or the active minority, from the governed or the power possessors. [4]

From this viewpoint, the illusive 'third force' enables the transition between systems and/or epochs yet it cannot come from within the components of the passive masses or the few in power. Instead, it acts from those individuals who are prepared and able to be vessels to transmit the spirit-consciousness through them and into material existence.

This is what has been termed as the 'Work' by various Traditions. It is the action of guided individuals and/or groups into behaviour, action, and attitude that can serve to bring into materiality certain specific forces required for the ongoing physical and metaphysical evolution of the planet and its inhabitants. Such people/ groups neither act as fully entangled within the exterior world nor fully extracted from it. As it is said, they are *in the world yet not of the world*. Through their presence, certain preparations can be made for the next phase of life; just as the mingled dualisms of light and dark continue

174

to form energies within the furnace of their contestations. Yet such people of the 'Work' aim to place themselves beyond these contestations through exhibiting a resonance distinct from the lower vibrations of the exterior world. Amidst the persistent and continuing hidden forces of life, a small number of human beings move in alignment with a greater Necessity.

References

[1] Bondarev, G.A. (1993) *Crisis of Civilization* (2nd Edition). Printed by Wellspring Bookshop: London, p137

[2] Cited in Gruwez, Christine (2014) *Mani & Rudolf Steiner*. Great Barrington, MA: SteinerBooks, p59

[3] Cited in Gruwez, Christine (2014) *Mani & Rudolf Steiner*. Great Barrington, MA: SteinerBooks, p60

[4] Cited in Author's notes – unknown source

The Will to Purpose (1):
Activating our Inner Drive & Intentionality

'A sincere reflection on human behavior is enough to convince us that the power of choice plays much less part in the life of man than we think.'

J.G. Bennett

We are familiar with the concept that a person has no real choice, and we generally regard this in relation to our commercial choices. That is, what we *choose* to buy is generally a decision based on a selection of limited choice. This has also been referred to as 'curated needs.' What we think or believe we want, or need, is conditioned into us – or 'curated' – so that we are merely responding to managed external stimuli to acquire certain goods. Whilst this is valid, and is indeed an operative modality, it remains within the material realm. In the opening citation, the thinker and author J.G. Bennett was referring to a form of choice beyond that of a material one. He was relating to the lack of choice within the inner world of the human being – that is, the presence of human will. Bennett was speaking and writing from the 1940s to the 1970s, yet what he said then is as relevant for today as he was not speaking about things that are relative to historical time or place but to an almost timeless situation – the human condition. The lack of genuine inner will of the human being has been made starker in modern times due to the lens of psychology and similar sciences. Professor Mattias Desmet has recently popularised the concept of mass formation and false solidarity, which refer to how crowd psychology is established and sustained.[44] In his recent book (*The Psychology of Totalitarianism*), Desmet points out that what we call totalitarianism has only been with us for the past 120 years, since the beginning of the twentieth century. Two previous examples that he gives are the Stalinist regime that came to power on the back of the Russian Revolution, and the National Socialist (Nazi) regime in Germany. Most recently, he says, the world is experiencing the rise of a global form of totalitarianism under the guise, or ideology, of technocracy. The one thing that totalitarianism has in common is that it is based on ideology rather than brute power. Further, that the populace is persuaded (or programmed) into obeyance through propaganda and social-cultural conditioning, rather than forced through fear (as is the case with dictatorships). The mass formation of willing obedience is a symbol for our times. With the availability of global

• • • • • • • • • • • •

44 See my previous essay: 'The Establishment of Mass Psychology & False Solidarity' - https://kingsleydennis.com/the-establishment-of-mass-psychology-false-solidarity/

communications, a largely digitally 'plugged-in' world population, the widespread influence of controlled media, and the pervasive presence of mind-influencing technologies, the human species has never been in a more pressing moment in its collective history.

Modern day humanity may not only be suffering from a lack of genuine choice; more importantly, it may be experiencing the dilemma of a lack of connection with internal will power. It is this dominant state of the human psyche – we may even go so far as to call it a widespread *psychosis* – that lies at the root of much of our present ills with its sense of apathy and pessimism. Some readers will be familiar with German philosopher Friedrich Nietzsche's concept of the *will to power*; lesser known is the English philosopher Colin Wilson and his notion of the *will to perceive*. For Wilson, the question of freedom and choice is not a social problem – it is an internal one for it requires an 'intensity of will.'[45] In other words, it is a personal struggle to achieve a form of self-awakening, or triggering, to arouse oneself from the torpidity and apathy of life. The issue is that for most people they don't consider the fragility of life's situation. The general masses, at least in the western world, consider themselves to be already free. They exist within the belief structure that they are protected and looked after by their governments

. . . .

45 For an in-depth study of Wilson's life and thought, I would recommend the excellent biography by Gary Lachman – *Beyond the Robot: The Life and Work of Colin Wilson* (2016)

and social institutions and that, give or take a few things, they have most essential needs provided for. Such people, I would posit, live on the outside of themselves – they are *skin-dwellers*. They live through their personalities and are most likely to adhere to mass consensus narratives. They are to be swayed by the rollercoaster ride of external events and react as anticipated by the governing elites who manipulate finances, food supply, energy supply, and more. This mass of people will only recognize the loss of freedom when it is threatened in relation to external events. It is a manufactured sense of freedom for once the threat has vanished – or seemingly made to vanish – then the meaning of freedom dissipates for the danger is no longer perceived. That is, it is an exterior crisis or danger that triggers people into action and as the perceived threat fades, they slip back once again into apathy and mass obedience. There is a lack of internal stimulation.

The stimulation of the human will requires that a person has the will to acquire insight. This they must choose for themselves, for no other agency shall give it to them. On the contrary, many social systems are designed to deteriorate a person's will by compelling them to give away their dependency and authority onto external systems. Consistency, commitment, and the *intention to will*, are human aspects severely undermined by the deliberate constraint of material structures and social systems. Such critical observations and the power of intention are also being increasingly undermined by the rise of what I would call 'lazy spirituality.' This is the type of Instagram positive thinking or *commercial well-beingness* that online 'spiritual celebrities' are all too eager to promote (and sell). Behind such on-demand spiritual well-being-positive-thinking packages is a passivity or laziness to critically engage in inner work and to gain perceptive cognition to recognize the fallacy inherent within the material domain. It is one thing to be positively-orientated and having 'oneness' for all creation; it is another matter to have the perceptive capacity to recognize that there are forces in play in the world that are active in nullifying metaphysical values and realities in order to replace them with an ever-deepening materialism. It would seem that there is an increasing form of cultural laziness and indecision, especially in this current time when people chiefly wish for things to be made easy for them. Instead of a person having faith and hope that they can change by making real effort, they are usually entertained with illusions that then take away from them the impulse to make any real change within themselves. In today's world, a person who seeks to develop inner awareness and to raise their perceptive capacity often find themselves at odds with their cultural milieu. Those with 'spiritual seriousness,' so to say, are what Colin Wilson referred to as the *Outsider*.[46] Such individuals have an intangible need to be more than just a 'happy, well-fed animal.' Again, Wilson referred to this state as being that of the robot; he said that we all have a robot within us that is eager to come out and take over all our daily duties for us. The Greek-Armenian mystic

· · · · · · · · · · · ·

46 See Colin Wilson's book *The Outsider* (originally published in 1956)

G.I. Gurdjieff called this the state of the 'man machine.' I have referred to this as the *robosapien*.[47]

Within such automated states the individual experiences the world through a narrowed lens of awareness. Wilson, for example, recognized that such limited awareness almost lulled a person into a 'state of permanent drowsiness, like being half-anesthetized' so that a broader vision of life is restricted. And this is how what we call ordinary, everyday life affects us. Whether it be through external impacts, stimulants, distractions, information, technological entanglement, energetic haze, and more, the environment of everyday life pacifies us by closing down our perceptual horizons. In response to this, Colin Wilson noted that 'it is as impossible to exercise freedom in an unreal world as it is to jump while you are falling.'[48] Freedom is not only related to physical mobility and access to human rights; it is also a question of an inner 'intensity of mind' that can pull a person out of the collective of mass formation (as Desmet would call it). Modern life can be regarded as a cause of spiritual decay because it seeks to demolish any recognition of a metaphysical reality. And through this, many people are unknowingly suffering a form of 'reality deficiency.' There have been people who, over the years, have strived to point this out to us, from wisdom teachers, mystics, and philosophers (like Colin

• • • • • • • • • • •

47 See my book *Hijacking Reality: The Reprogramming and Reorganization of Human Life* (2021)

48 Wilson, Colin (1982) *The Outsider*. Los Angeles: Jeremy P. Tarcher, p39

Wilson). This deficiency prevents people from receiving inner nourishment; over time, this acts to deprive human cognition by literally starving it of nutrients (perception). We are in a time right now of great 'reality deficiency' as the dominant consensus narratives peddle their lies, manipulations, and programming.

Each age has its own form of reality and/or metaphysical suppression, from the physically overt (Spanish Inquisition) to the covert (technocracy). Within each specific era, there are calculated forces that act to impinge upon the individuals' own evolutionary drive toward not only self-attainment but, more importantly, a connection with a transcendental impulse (what some may call as Source). The historian Arnold Toynbee believed that civilizations (and its individuals) progress by overcoming struggles; by moving through 'challenge points,' so to speak. If the crisis is too great, the civilization succumbs and collapses. If the challenge is not great enough, the civilization overcomes and becomes complacent, slides into greater decadence and eventually collapses. The challenge must be just right – the 'Goldilocks' zone, as Gary Lachman calls it. Challenges bring out the best in individuals too, yet they must be able to grow and develop through the crisis – and this is often down to an *inner will* or drive. Toynbee believed that a civilization needs to pro-duce a 'creative minority' to meet such a challenge of its time. It would seem that we are amidst such a 'challenge point' right now; and it is not only a physical crisis but also an existential one. I would go further and suggest that human civilization cannot survive indefinitely without some inborn sense of a transcendental purpose – otherwise it is like a hollow shell that becomes increasingly brittle over time. British philosopher and historian Nicholas Hagger, whose monumental work *The Fire and the Stones* examines the sacred impulse (the 'Fire/Light') within twenty-five civilizations, likewise has shown how civilizations are inspired by the transcendental impulse and decay when such an impulse is forgotten or dismissed.[49]

What is required is for us, our communities and cultures, to become more conscious of our participation in reality. Further, that what we take to be reality is a merger between the physical and the metaphysical. As such, humanity is a being 'of spirit' that is manifesting through the intermediary of a physical body. To take this even further, we need to come to recognize that all existence is consciousness primarily, and that physical phenomena is an energetic state that manifests from a source of consciousness. What is required of humanity to survive beyond this existential crisis and challenge point is to become *more conscious*. Is this possible? Colin Wilson was not so sure. Wilson believed, and stated as such, that the majority of people cannot accept the burden of becoming more conscious. He felt that the 'masses' were both consciously and subconsciously choosing the more comfortable 'mediocracy of life.' I would even question

· · · · · · · · · · · ·

49 Hagger, Nicholas (1991) *The Fire and the Stones*. Dorset: Element Books.

what this term means any more – what is the 'mediocracy of life' when we can no longer be sure what reality is? Abstractions have now replaced realities to create an enveloping world of pseudo-reality and a 'theatre of the absurd.' As I talked about in my book *Bardo Times*,[50] life has become a simulation – a simulacra as the French theorist Jean Baudrillard would say – and the notion of what is 'real' appears to have dissolved into what is the latest consensus narrative. What *is* important to acknowledge in these challenging times is that as the chaos whirls around us, humanity stands on the threshold of a higher form of life.

This is the other point that perceptive individuals have been attempting to point out to us (not least of them has been the Indian sage Sri Aurobindo). And this threshold becomes more apparent and urgent whenever a civilization begins either its decline or its necessary transition to a different epoch and modality. This is the challenge that civilization must face – either to raise/adjust its level of consciousness and perceptive capacity or stagnate and then collapse. Human civilization necessarily reflects the state of perception of its inhabitants. As that indwelling perception expands, so too does the physical environment develop in alignment. If perceptive capacity is restricted or even being deliberately reduced, as is the case right now, then entropic or atrophying forces begin to dominate.

• • • • • • • • • • • • •

50 *Bardo Times: hyperreality, high-velocity, simulation, automation, mutation - a hoax?* (2018)

This is why we must resist, at great effort, to submit to a programming of conformity and perceptive limitation that is likely to come about through increased technocratic forms of social management and control. This is where Colin Wilson's notion of the *will to perceive* comes in. Due to the external environment, human consciousness is generally conditioned into a dulled state so that higher insights or perceptions are not 'allowed' to get through. We need to seek to 'widen' (expand) our consciousness beyond such limiting influences so that greater perceptive insights can be achieved. Most people, however, are reflections of their surroundings and, as such, require external inputs to motivate or trigger them into action. Chaos and crises can function as such triggering impacts. The 'will to perceive' also activates a *will to purpose*. Behind the human developmental impulse there is a push, I would say, to increase our intentionality. Without the 'will to purpose' there is a lack of conscious participation. It is the *will to purpose* that distinguishes the human being from the machine – the 'robosapien.' Modern life, with its technocratic pull, is encouraging people not to think but to allow automation to take over duties and responsibilities. On the contrary, we need to be 'pulling ourselves up by the bootstraps' and intentionally driving ourselves across the threshold. What could this threshold be?

Humanity is moving towards a stage in its evolutionary path whereby it becomes cognizant of its role as a fusion (a bridge or merger) between spirit/consciousness and physicality/matter. We are, in these times, the forward ground crew sent ahead to prepare the groundwork. Sometime in the future – it could be ten, twenty, thirty years or more – human understanding and the sciences will come to recognize the primary role of consciousness behind all existence. And when this occurs, human life will alter drastically. We shall understand that human existence is a merging of non-physical intelligence with physical forces. The very notion of life and reality will be greatly expanded beyond current conceptions. We shall be propelled beyond the confines of the physical robot – the *robosapien* – and shall utilize presently unknown organs of perception. But we are not at that threshold yet. And this is partly why we are seeing a contestation of forces in play. There are forces that do not wish for humanity to reach, and pass, this threshold for we shall then no longer be their passive robots to manage and control. The present control hierarchies will be demolished. And there is a small contingency that wish to cut humanity off from this transcendental impulse, to isolate us from receiving such developmental forces, and to push us back into our perceptual prisons of the 'everyday mundane.' Such forces aim to increase the programming and technologies of cognitive influence to hypnotize the mass of humanity into accepting an 'upside-down' reality that the robosapien seems the most suited to. Our *will to purpose* now is about having the inner drive and intentionality to move us beyond this current predicament and modern state of alienation, and forward into a state of heightened cognition and expanded perceptual awareness.

It is my view that the 'teething pains' that we are presently experiencing represent the birthing, or arrival, of a new form of consciousness coming to manifestation through the human species. That is, a mergence with an expanded field of consciousness. And for this to emerge, the individual is called upon to 'meet it' halfway, so to speak. Social forces will attempt to continue to hold back the individual by mental, emotional, and physical/ biological interventions. And yet, against these artificial constrictions, I am confident that if enough of us (we don't need to be a majority) can strive for cognitive freedom, perceptive clarity, and inner awareness, we can become the early wave – the *evolutionary outsider* – to make the initial steps across the threshold. Just enough of us need to act as the 'antennae of the race'[51] to pass the baton onto our descendants. And that, I would say, gives us enough reason to activate our *will to purpose.*

· · · · · · · · · · · ·

51 A phrase coined by the poet Ezra Pound.

The Will to Purpose (2):
Activating the Metaphysical Inner Drive

When someone's ideas begin to provide a less-than-adequate support for his sense of individual integrity and group cohesion, we get a reshaping of them around a new or improved concept: again, if he or she is not psychologically autonomous.

Idries Shah, *A Perfumed Scorpion*

In the preceding essay,[52] I talked about how an effort is required – a *will-to-purpose* – so that insight can be acquired and take a person away from automated behaviour. That is, away from the state of the 'robosapien.' The exercise of such purpose-driven will is a conscious act, an attempt to break out of conditioned traits, opinions, and the consensus narrative. It is the will to acquire insight, and to perceive those societal conditions that push people to conform and to place their dependency and authority onto external systems. Yet, at the same time, such a purposeful will can be a conscious, secular inner drive, based on rational cognition. It need not be related to

• • • • • • • • • • • •

52 *The Will to Purpose: Activating our Inner Drive & Intentionality*

an inner impulse or a metaphysical impulse. There is a distinct lack of support in modern societies for pursuing the inner life, and for the inner quest. The denial of the inner life is reflected through increasing materialism; and these material forces then influence and shape the life of the inner spirit or force. The inner life becomes what it is fed upon. And if it is fed upon nothingness? The outer life may be dotted and interspersed with glamorous distractions and entertainments, whilst the inner life exists in a dark void. In order for a metaphysical inner drive, a shift in perception is required, which then alters how consciousness interprets local reality. This shift inaugurates a new centre of insight that recognizes the metaphysical principles that underlie reality and our physical existence. Some people, such as Nicholas Hagger, refer to this awakening perception as akin to a 'Heracleitus' Fire' that unites spiritual and physical outlooks.[53]

The metaphysical perspective seeks awareness of the greater reality beyond/behind the physical world (the prefix 'meta' can mean both 'beyond' as well as 'behind'). In other words, it is the eternal behind the temporal. What is being referred to here are those aspects beyond surface appearances. The immaterial fire, or light, exists as the metaphysical background (radiation) to physical existence; and it radiates, or flows, into physicality through material bodies/forms. That is, the metaphysical light *infuses*

· · · · · · · · · · · ·

53 See *A Metaphysical's Way of Fire: Collected Poems* by Nicholas Hagger

materiality through a vital force of energy, or conscious will power. This non-visible metaphysical fire/light is not perceived by the outer senses, but by the inner being. For this reason, it remains untouchable to the persona, or social ego, of the individual. It can be communed with through inner effort, or through the receptivity of one's being; yet it remains beyond the grasping senses of the superficial person. It is the controlling social ego – the social personality – that dictates most peoples' everyday lives. The 'will-to-purpose' that is focused upon these external matters may drive a person further into materiality; and thus, further distanced from a metaphysical reality.

The deepening materiality of our modern era has further dissolved the presence and recognition of metaphysical impulses in human life. It has also strived to create societies devoid of metaphysical impulses. The 'will-to-purpose' is an aspect of the Creative Imagination that works through an integrated brain hemisphere, rather than being trapped within a materialistic, analytical, cortical, left-brain. The creative imagination suffuses the individual's inner being rather than being a product of the interpreting social ego/persona. Along with the creative imagination there is the Intuitive Intellect that operates beyond the veil of a rationalized, conditioned intellect. Art, literature, symbols, and the like, can act as portals or gateways for the transmission of metaphysical information into human cultures and societies. In recent years, this medium of transmission has become overtly visual alongside a dumbing down of textual materials.

Fewer and fewer people are gaining knowledge and/or information through books and written texts, especially the younger generation. The immersion into textual materials takes time, effort, and attention; contrary to the now famous 'sound bites' realm of social media, twitterings, 'insta-influencers,' and similar superficial and exploitative modes of expression.

The process of transmutation and transformation takes an amount of intentional 'will-to-purpose' aligned with a metaphysical inner drive that is less coveted by our modern cultures. In fact, it can be said that this innate sense of longing that is an aspect of the inner being, and the disquietude and dissatisfaction that can come from this, is often channelled into other superficial needs and temporary social satisfiers. Such 'social satisfiers' act as a form of conversion therapy that attaches people to dependency-orientated activities and habits as a way of providing comfort and reassurance, which people then become overly used to. Metaphysical symbols and vocabulary (the 'transmitters') have lost their precision and/or function in modern times. Many of them have become slogans, branding, and mostly 'dead language' as they have been co-opted by superficial organizations and groups. Language such as: 'heart;' 'spirit;' 'psyche;' 'eternal;' 'self;' 'soul;' 'transcendence;' 'cosmos;' and many others have become co-opted and colonized by a commercial, materialistic, and often exploitative energy. The patterns of metaphysical meaning and significance that such language once weaved, has been deactivated by a modern social language that vibrates with a flat frequency of materialistic pseudo-spirituality. Perhaps the way forward now is to frame such aspects within a psychological understanding, utilizing a psycho-spiritual lens of perception.

Psychologically Autonomous

To talk about activating the 'metaphysical inner drive' we have to recognize the necessity to dissolve those ties or attachments that prevent further development. These ties often include an over-reliance upon too many of these superficial 'social satisfiers.' If people remain within these lower order satisfiers, then they are less likely to be compelled or driven towards possibilities beyond their present state. If this initial energy, drive, or capacity is not found, then it is unlikely there will be a reason to reach towards such possibilities. A person cannot be compelled through insincere, ingenuine, or forced reasons and impulses. This would only be a case of the reprogramming of beliefs – replacing one belief set with another. What I am referring to here as the metaphysical inner drive requires that the individual displays a sufficient degree of psychological autonomy. That is, they have reached a stage where they are sufficiently detached from their previous states of social conditioning that are acquired during the normal course of their upbringing and maturing years. It is a sign of our times that few people consider the state of their own psychological condition or even question the notion of psychological autonomy – or whether such autonomy is good or even possible.

The general human psyche becomes attached to those impacts and influences that touch them emotionally, or which they like or are excited by. Yet these are the very impulses which, most of the time, are the type of influences least needed. The regular inner drive can be fuelled and energized by following particular likes and personal orientations. However, the metaphysical inner drive is more likely to require input and stimulation from those impulses not immediately recognizable as such, and which are often far away from entertaining and emotionally attractive. As it is said, such influences are more likely to find the person when they are ready for contact, rather than the person finding the contact through their own means when still within a conditioned state. As it has been noted:

> We may at once admit that cultures which seek to highlight crudities, things which immediately appeal, and to project them in attractive forms and endorse and sustain them are unlikely to produce, on the whole, people with appetites for other than more of the same thing.[1]

These appetites that have been shaped for crudities – the superficial 'social satisfiers' – are likely to perpetuate the same behaviours within people that feed these desires. The recognition of this is part of the first stage in shifting to a will-to-purpose that is internally driven. For many, this will offer a formidable barrier to surmount. And it can be surmounted, if the phenomena and its associated behaviour traits can be observed in action; and then conscious action taken to comprehend these influences and impacts. It is no use to immerse oneself in commercial systems of well-being – such are nowadays classed as 'spiritual pursuits' – and then to wonder why no real progress has been achieved. As the saying goes: reading does not change people unless they are ready to change.

The metaphysical inner drive is not an impulse for well-being or 'spiritual satisfaction.' It is an inner impulse for heightened perception, understanding, and ultimately knowledge concerning the human condition and humankind's role in this reality. The person of inner perceptual understanding is able to stand aside from the context of their environment, so that it has minimal effect on them, yet also blending with it when required. It is the superficial 'will-to-purpose' that seeks to dominate the environment and those within it – yet it is this style of behaviour that is both encouraged by consensus society as well as rewarded by it. This is the distraction onto transient things as if they were constant. The will-to-purpose of the metaphysical inner drive seeks to take the individual out of, and beyond, the constraints of a life in which they have no understanding of or control over. Without this metaphysical perception and comprehension, a person remains bound within the limitations of what is sometimes referred to as an 'accidental life.' This can be described as:

> 'He does not live very long, he can control very little of his circumstances, and the things which happen to him, even in the most highly structured environments, may have far more effect on his life than the things which he causes to happen: however much he may strive, and irrespective of whether or not he believes the reverse to be true. [2]

In order to change their state of consciousness, a person may first need to face the situation of their physical reality. The core of the current situation is that whilst humanity may collectively be experiencing a moral, political, financial, and existential crisis, this is not the central crux. The essential characteristic of these times is that humanity is experiencing an evolutionary crisis. This is why so many aspects of our lives appear either broken or in breakdown. All that has once been splendid is now in disarray and dissolution. And yet without these multiple breakdowns and death throes, human consciousness will not gain the impetus to shift into another perceptual state. And it is the metaphysical inner drive that will not only assist this transformation but also will be better suited to the future post-transition. Furthermore, it is this transformative process that is currently creating such an intense anxiety within the world. We may ask ourselves: when everything collapses, what remains?

Without sufficient insight, all focus gets placed upon the transient and the superficial. These are the external factors that hook and pull people into a controlling consensus reality with very limited understanding. In this condition, little or nothing is known about the processes unfolding within our reality. Without understanding, people are quickly drawn into analysing, criticising, and commenting upon external factors that are several steps removed from the metaphysical truths of what are occurring in our environments. It is the will-to-purpose of the metaphysical impulse that can stop a person from being manipulated and suffocated under conditions they do not understand. By not comprehending these external processes and their influences, people can be drawn into states of anxiety, frustration, and anger. As the saying goes: Did the philosophy of the fish ever help it to become an amphibian?' This is why there is much to be said about gaining one's psychological autonomy, which is disengaged from the persistent conditioning and programming of the exterior world. The real catastrophe of our times is not the upheaval and chaos that plague our societies, or the criminal acts of the psychopathic 'elite' few, but that the human individual is being lured away from the potentials of their own innate creative forces and into a state of servitude. Now is the time not only for perceptive cognition of the forces operative in our world but also for activating the metaphysical inner drive within enough receptive individuals. What is needed is transformative change.

Permanent transformative change is what transfigures the human 'being' rather than just talking endlessly about consciousness and methods for attaining so-called 'higher' consciousness (not that consciousness was ever a vertical property!). To transfigure the human individual (establish a new, developed state) marks a difference between a world of ideas (mental and/or emotional) and a world that is perceived and comprehended from a distinct degree of perceptive understanding. Modern life is largely cultivated from the world of ideas rather than a world conducive to metaphysical truths. Thus, modern life only accumulates upon the externals, but does not utilize its resources for the possibility of transmutation. This systematic and consistent accumulation ultimately becomes a burden upon an energetically heavy, materialistic world. Similarly, any form of psychology cut off from an inner vitality and spirit is ultimately materialistic. What is required is a recognition of, and contact with, a psycho-spirit vital energy, and not just separate disciplines of 'spirituality' and 'psychology' – but both to work on the inner being. It is this lack of a psychological approach to inner work that has allowed many current practices of 'spirituality' to drift into a commercial 'well-being' marketplace that caters for those seeking easily absorbed 'spirit satisfiers.' What is necessary now is for enough able body-minded people to work towards the *potentialization of the human condition* before human civilization either is dragged into a technocratic transhumanist future or falls into a mire of spiritual wishful thinking.

References

[1] Shah, Idries, (1978) *A Perfumed Scorpion.* London: Octagon Press, p.138-9

[2] Shah, Idries, (1978) *A Perfumed Scorpion.* London: Octagon Press, p.140

Illusion & Truth:
The Disintegration of Metaphysical Values

"Yes, the world is an illusion. But Truth is always being
shown there."

Idries Shah, *The Dermis Probe.*

It seems that we can talk about consciousness and
consciousness studies so long as it remains within the
'reality remit' and does not push against the 'barriers
of perception.' This is why so much of our modern
societies and the media marketplace are filled with pop-
spirituality as they function as cultural remedies rather
than revolutions. That is, they provide a band aid plaster
rather than seeking to find a permanent cure. Many easy
'self-help' practices offer a 'false exit' revolving door so
that people are given the sensation of finding a way out
of the 'system' only to be brought back into it again. Such
teachings or offerings act as *auto-tranquilizers* – they act as
auto-tranquilizing mechanisms to provide an alternative
treatment, or pleasing sensation, that appears as fringe or
'outside' the system but is not. Rather, it is another sub-

set within the overall program; but a subset that does not constitute a threat or provide a means to perceive through the programmed reality set. In other words, it is an *allowed anomaly*.

The 'allowed anomalies' are examples of mechanisms of mental anesthesia that soften or even dispel the original urge to seek for answers. They also serve as a quick satiation (fast food) to bring temporary satisfaction. Temporary satiation, or satisfaction, dulls down the real hunger so that afterwards the developmental urge remains in the 'goldilocks zone' of not too hungry or too full – just full enough to want to keep on with the spiritual pursuit yet not too hungry that they wish to seek beyond what is openly offered or available in the marketplace. The forces currently acting upon humanity are those that shall compel us to *die away* or *die to become*. The opportunity now available compels us to become something qualitatively new. This is now the perfect time for personal advancement and for the expansion of perception and awareness. It is no longer necessary to be clever – it is essential to be wise.

There has been a noticeable decline in what, in simple terms, may be called the 'metaphysical quest' (what has also been known as the 'spiritual quest'). The inner impulse to seek beyond material-physical appearances has almost vanished from contemporary life. It was long ago co-opted into religious pursuits and fashioned into ritualistic ceremonies and dogma. And more recently, it has been ushered into what I have previously called 'Ashram Avenues' and 'Guru Boulevards' by people enticed with exotic interests. The glamour of 'self-development' has found a wanting marketplace within the glare of social media. The depth of inner longing is scratched at the surface and satisfied by sipping at the singing bowls of inner harmony and world peace.

It is all too easy to become stereotypes of ourselves, driven by platitudes of false mysticism and superficial attainment. There is so much within contemporary life that bears down upon us to make us forget ourselves that just the act of self-remembering becomes a force of rebellion and treason against the material world. We are led to forget those capacities that we bring with us from the metaphysical realm. We are here in this world as both guests and custodians; we inhabit our bodies during the life experience in the hope of making the most of those gifted lives. And yet, we rarely come to realize the truth of who we really are. We become entranced by the material realm and its systemic diversions. Our independent liberty and free will is dismantled by succumbing to set patterns, habits, and programmed behaviours. Generally, in our societies an individual is 'permitted' to access a form of 'spirituality' just enough to provide them with a taster smell of satisfaction. This is then carried around throughout life as a constant marker of 'satisfied attainment' – an outer recognized badge of honour. The individual then stops doing the Work – the critical seeking – and falls into line within the Game. The perennial memory starts to fade again. Yet ... have we ever done enough?

Human civilization is infected with deviant distractions distributed through social, cultural, and also spiritual mischief. So much false gold within circulation creates a parallel economy. On the other side, however, true gold increases its value. The disintegration of metaphysical values, and the moral decay that accompanies this, are part of a deliberate projection into hyper-materialism. We have yet to fully realize that the fastest way to awaken is to become the cause of someone else's awakening. By assisting and serving our fellow human beings we are simultaneously helping ourselves. Many people are already awake – they just don't know it yet. Sounds contradictory? How many times have we known that something is the right thing to do and yet we fail to do it? Similarly, so many people instinctively feel the inner urge, and sense the inversion of the world, and yet choose not to act upon this. In the words of the sage and philosopher Sri Aurobindo:

> At first the inner consciousness seems to be
> the dream and the outer the waking reality.
> Afterwards the inner consciousness becomes
> the reality and the outer is felt by many as
> a dream or delusion, or else as something
> superficial and external.[54]

. . . .

54 Sri Aurobindo, *Integral Yoga*. Lotus Press (1993), p49

Our current consensus reality is not an accurate portrayal of the life experience, and it is no longer where we need to be. We need to turn things around so that the outer world is recognized to be the dream state, or the lower perceptive level of reality. It is time to choose a different timeline – if that makes any sense?

If people continue to be fed by the dross of the external world – its media circus, entertainment absurdities, and directed propaganda – then the consensus reality gets continually imprinted (validated) by these inputs that people feed back into the system. A new template or consciousness field struggles to come into existence. The mass perceptive state remains low – very low. And as a collective species, humanity can no longer remain at this low level of perceptive awareness (ignorance) at a time when an advancement in awareness is vital. It is simply not sustainable in the long term. If this polarized state continues, then there is likely to be a splintering in humanity's future, and not everyone will walk the same path going forward. What we choose today will become the reality we shall experience later. Now is the time for advancement in terms of perceptive awareness: it is time to EXPAND. It is time to grow out of the lens of infantile perception. It is time to walk each step with awareness, with conscious knowing, instead of stumbling through on autopilot.

Let us ponder on our predicament by concluding with the following tale:

THE FRUIT OF THE TREE

An ancient tale tells how a wise man once related a story about a remarkable tree which was to be found in India. People who ate of the fruit of this tree, as he told it, would neither grow old nor die. This legend was repeated, by a reliable person, to one of the Central Asian kings of long ago, and this monarch at once conceived a passionate desire for the fruit – the source of the Elixir of Life.

So the King sent a suitably resourceful representative to find and to bring back the fruit of that tree. For many years the emissary visited one city after another, travelled all over India, town and country, and diligently asked about the object of his search from anyone who might know about its nature and where it was to be found.

As you can imagine, some people told this man that such a search must obviously only be a madman's quest; others questioned him closely to find out how a person of such evident intelligence could actually be involved in such an absurd adventure; their kindness in this respect, showing their consideration for him as a deluded dupe, hurt him even more than the physical blows which the ignorant had also rained upon him.

Many people, of course, told him false tales, sending him from one destination to another, claiming that they, too, had heard of the miraculous Tree. Years passed in this way, until the King's representative lost all his hope of success, and made the decision to return to the royal court and confess his dismal failure. Now, there was also, luckily, a certain man of real wisdom in India - they do occasionally exist there - and the King's man, having heard of him late in his search, thought; 'I will at least go to him, desperate as I am, to seek his blessing on my journey homeward.'

He went to the wise man, and asked him for a blessing, and he explained how it was that he had got into such a distressed condition, a failure without hope. The sage laughed and explained:

'You simpleton; you don't need a blessing half as much as you need orientation. Wisdom is the fruit of the Tree of Knowledge. Because you have taken images and form, secondary names for things, as your aim, you have not been able to find what lies beyond. It has thousands of names: it may be called the Water of Life, the Sun, an Ocean and even a Cloud ... But the emblem is not the thing itself.'

Whoever, this Teacher continued, attaches himself to names and clings to concepts without being able to see that these derivative things are only stages, sometimes barriers, to understanding, will stay at the stage of secondary things. They create, and remain in a sub-culture of emotional stimulus, fantasy and quasi-religion.[55]

• • • • • • • • • • • • •

55 Idries Shah, (1978) *A Perfumed Scorpion*. London: Octagon Press, p137-8